The TOP 100 New Orleans RECIPES of all time

The TOP 100 New Orleans RECIPES of all time

Compiled by
John DeMers
and
Rhonda Findley

Acadian House
PUBLISHING
Lafayette, Louisiana

ISBN 0-925417-51-3

♦ Published by Acadian House Publishing, Lafayette, Louisiana.
  (Edited by Trent Angers; interior graphic design and production
  by Jon Russo.)

♦ Cover design and production by Elizabeth Bell, Lafayette, Louisiana

♦ Printed by Phoenix Color Corp., Hagerstown, Maryland, USA

INTRODUCTION
Great Food Is Part
Of New Orleans' Heritage

It's a strange day in each New Orleanian's life when he or she realizes people travel great distances to eat here. Some even come from overseas.

"Come on," we ask, "really?"

And the answer we get is, "Yes, really."

This may come as a mild surprise to many New Orleanians because we're so used to eating delicious foods, day in and day out, in our homes, in neighborhood cafés, and occasionally in the city's fine restaurants. It would be fair to say that we New Orleanians take our local cuisine for granted.

Good food is said to be Louisiana's number one tourist attraction, and nowhere in the state is there more of a concentration of top-flight restaurants serving such food than in the Greater New Orleans area.

Visitors come from New York, San Francisco and Miami. They fly in from London, Paris and Quebec. They enjoy fine dining at Antoine's, Brennan's, Commander's Palace, and Alex Patout's. They compliment the chefs on dishes such as Oysters Rockefeller, Trout Amandine, Shrimp Remoulade and Bananas Foster.

Recipes for these and many other foods served in the city's fine restaurants can be found in the pages of this cookbook.

But, the majority of recipes in the book are simply for home cooking. They are recipes used for preparing the everyday foods that are regularly cooked by and consumed by the people of New Orleans and the surrounding area.

For example, Shrimp Creole, Red Beans & Rice, Jambalaya, Lasagna, Meatball Po-boys, Oyster Loaves, Muffaletta Sandwiches, Chicken & Sausage Gumbo, Smothered Greens, *Maque Choux*, Fried Chicken, Fried Green Tomatoes, Boiled Crabs, "Dirty Rice," Corn Bread, Blackberry

Cobbler and Pecan Pralines.

Like the great foods of any other major city in the world, New Orleans cuisine is the result of contributions from many people, from many cultures, over many generations. The French, Spanish, Cajuns, Sicilians and African-Americans were and continue to be very influential in the creation of New Orleans foods. Others influencing the cuisine include Native American Indians, the Irish, Cubans and Vietnamese.

This book is the result of a major effort to round up, as the title says, the top 100 New Orleans recipes of all time – the real classics of New Orleans cooking. We are reasonably confident that after considering hundreds of candidates we have compiled the top 100. We believe that if another such list were to be drawn up in, say, 100 years, most of the recipes in this book would be included. Only time will tell.

– John DeMers

ACKNOWLEDGEMENTS

Quite a number of people gave of their time and knowledge to make this book a reality. We are particularly indebted to the following for their contributions:

The many New Orleanians and others who shared their recipes for this project, whose names you will find throughout the book.

Our panel of experts who helped identify the top 100 New Orleans recipes, namely, Angela Cocke of McIlhenny Company's Marketing Division; Albert Charlton and Frank Donaldson, both of whom are good cooks and lifelong residents of the New Orleans area; Ella Brennan of Commander's Palace; Tom Pittari Jr. of T. Pittari's Restaurant (1895-1984); cookbook author Holly Clegg; and veteran Louisiana food writer Sandra Day.

The staff of Acadian House Publishing, including Trent Angers, the editor, who had the foresight to get this project going and the tenacity to see it through; and Neal Bertrand (a.k.a. "Eagle Eye"), who proofread every word in the book, more than once, and found and cleaned up errors that the average eye might miss.

– J.D. and R.F.

PHOTO AND ART CREDITS

The photographs in this book were provided by the Louisiana Office of Tourism.

The drawings in the book were done by Tom Sommers of Crowley, La.

Two Basic Recipes Important in New Orleans Cooking

Roux

- 4 tablespoons of oil
- 6 tablespoons of flour

1. Heat oil in pot; add flour, stirring constantly over medium-high heat until brown.

2. Lower heat and continue cooking and stirring until dark brown.

Some of the recipes in this edition vary, but these are the basic proportions of oil to flour. Specific quantities differ with the different recipes, of course.

Rice

- 1 cup of rice
- 2 cups of water
- 1 tablespoon of oil or butter
- 1 teaspoon of salt

1. Put all ingredients in a two-quart saucepan and bring to a boil.

2. Lower heat to medium and cook until rice and water are at the same level.

3. Cover, lower heat to low and cook 20 minutes.

4. Remove from heat and let stand for five to ten minutes before serving.

Another way to measure the proportions of rice to water is to add enough water to the pan to cover the rice by the depth of one finger joint (index finger). This rule applies no matter how much rice you're cooking.

TABLE OF CONTENTS

The TOP 100 New Orleans RECIPES of all time

Café du Monde, across from Jackson Square,
serves world-famous beignets and coffee.

Pain Perdu

We love the name the French hung on this version of French toast. Realizing this recipe is great with bread that's getting old and dry, they called the dish pain perdu – *lost bread.*

- 1/2 teaspoon of vanilla extract
- 1/2 cup of milk
- 2 tablespoons of sugar
- 1/2 teaspoon of ground nutmeg
- 3 eggs
- 1/8 teaspoon of salt
- 10 slices of stale French bread, about one inch thick
- 3 tablespoons of butter
- Powdered sugar and/or syrup

1. In a mixing bowl, whisk together vanilla, milk, sugar, nutmeg, eggs and salt.

2. Soak bread in this mixture until thoroughly coated and saturated, five to seven minutes.

3. In a large sauté pan, melt a tablespoon of butter over medium-high heat. Add three or four pieces of French bread and brown on both sides, about five minutes.

4. Repeat this process until all bread is cooked.

5. Serve on a warm plate and drizzle with powdered sugar or syrup.

Serves five.

– Jen Plourde
French Quarter, New Orleans

15

Beignets

Just try telling New Orleanians that going to the French Market for beignets is only for the tourists! But don't try enjoying these powdered-sugary fried doughnuts while wearing dark clothes, unless you want to look like you just came in from a blizzard.

- 1 cup of scalded milk
- 2 tablespoons of vegetable oil
- 1 egg, beaten
- 2 tablespoons of sugar
- 1 envelope of dry yeast
- 3 cups of flour
- 1 teaspoon of salt
- ½ teaspoon of ground cinnamon
- ½ teaspoon of ground nutmeg
- Vegetable oil
- Powdered sugar

1. In a large bowl, combine the milk with the two tablespoons of vegetable oil, egg and the sugar. Blend thoroughly.

2. Add the dry yeast and stir to dissolve.

3. Sift together the flour, salt and spices, then add this mixture to the yeast mixture.

4. Form a large ball of dough, return it to the bowl, cover the bowl with a towel, and allow time for the dough to double in bulk, about 20 minutes. Then punch down and knead until dough is elastic.

5. On a floured board, roll out the dough to one-fourth-inch thickness and cut into four-inch squares. Cover and allow to rise again, about 45 minutes.

6. Pour three inches of vegetable oil into a deep fryer and heat to 375 degrees.

16

7. Drop in dough squares a few at a time, cooking and turning them until golden.

8. Remove with a slotted spoon and drain on absorbent paper.

9. Dust with powdered sugar.

10. Serve hot, three per person, to start.

Serves eight.

Café au Lait

The general plan for café au lait *in New Orleans (as served round the clock at Café du Monde, across from Jackson Square) involves coffee that's brewed stronger than would ever be appreciated by one of those chains from someplace like Seattle, plus lots of milk that's piping hot and frothy.*

- 32 ounces of strongly brewed coffee and chicory (Suggested brands include *Café Du Monde* Coffee and Chicory or Community Coffee and Chicory blend. Both are made in Louisiana.)
- 32 ounces of whole milk, piping hot
- Sugar

1. Brew coffee according to directions on the package.

2. In a small saucepan over low heat, warm the milk. Be careful to stir and not to scald.

3. Pour hot coffee in mugs, filling half way only.

4. Add milk to top. Mixture should be half milk, half coffee.

5. Sweeten to taste.

Grillades & Grits

Veal used to be the poor man's choice of meat around New Orleans, as shown by the fact that breaded veal cutlets were long known as nothing more specific than "panéed meat." Such is hardly the case anymore, of course. But one of the city's favorite brunch dishes remains this classic pairing of veal with grits beneath a blanket of savory, tomato-kissed sauce. This is a big hit in the wee hours of many Mardi Gras balls.

- 2 pounds of veal cutlets, trimmed
- ½ cup of vegetable oil
- 4½ teaspoons of salt
- 2½ teaspoons of white sugar
- 1 teaspoon of black pepper
- Sauce (Recipe follows)
- Grits (Recipe follows)
- Green onions, for garnish (optional)

1. Cut veal into 3x3-inch medallions and pound with a mallet to flatten.

2. Heat oil on medium-high heat in a large sauté pan.

3. Combine the salt, sugar and pepper.

4. Season the cutlets and sauté until browned on both sides, about two minutes.

5. Remove from pan and set aside while preparing the Sauce.

6. Add veal cutlets to Sauce and cook covered on low heat about 30 minutes, until veal is tender.

7. To serve, spoon about one-half cup of grits onto plate, off center. Spoon grillades and Sauce half of the way on top of grits and onto plate. Garnish with green onions if you like.

SAUCE

- 1 cup of bacon grease or vegetable oil
- 1 cup of all-purpose flour
- 1 quart of veal stock or water
- 1/8 teaspoon of white pepper
- 1/8 teaspoon of cayenne pepper
- 1/8 teaspoon of black pepper
- 1 teaspoon of salt
- 3 tablespoons of butter
- 1 cup of julienned white onion
- 1 cup of julienned bellpepper
- 1 cup of julienned celery
- 1 tablespoon of minced garlic
- 1 cup of sliced mushrooms
- 1 cup of peeled, seeded and diced tomatoes

1. Heat bacon grease in a four-quart heavy pot, stir-in flour and cook on medium heat, stirring constantly to make a dark roux.

2. Add veal stock, white pepper, cayenne pepper, black pepper and salt and stir well. Bring to a boil, reduce heat and simmer 20 to 30 minutes.

3. In a separate medium sauté pan, heat butter on moderate heat. Add onion, bellpepper, celery and garlic and cook three minutes.

4. Add mushrooms and tomatoes and cook about two minutes.

5. Add this vegetable mixture to the Sauce and stir.

GRITS

- 4 cups of water
- ½ teaspoon of salt
- 1 cup of instant golden grits
- 4 tablespoons of butter

1. Bring water to a boil, then add salt and slowly stir-in grits.

2. Reduce heat, add butter and cook five to seven minutes.

Serves four to six.

– The Court of Two Sisters
French Quarter, New Orleans

Eggs Sardou

They say the quintessential Eggs Sardou is found at Antoine's Restaurant, the creators of this classic New Orleans recipe named for Victorien Sardou, a famous French playwright. Some variations contain anchovies and truffles. But, you'll always find artichoke hearts and hollandaise in the classic preparation when dining in any of New Orleans' fine restaurants.

CREAMED SPINACH

- 2 cups of fresh spinach, cooked and drained then chopped fine
- 1 cup of Béchamel Sauce (Recipe follows)
- ¼ teaspoon of salt
- ½ teaspoon of freshly ground black pepper

1. In a small saucepan over medium heat, combine the Béchamel Sauce with the spinach. Add salt and pepper.

2. Stir to fully incorporate all of the ingredients and to heat through. Set aside.

BÉCHAMEL SAUCE

- 8 ounces of butter
- 4 ounces of all-purpose flour
- 2 quarts of milk
- 2 teaspoons of salt

1. Melt butter in a medium-size saucepan over medium heat. Slowly add flour to make a roux, stirring constantly to work out any lumps. Cook for five minutes only, to make a white roux.

2. In a separate saucepan, heat milk on medium heat. Avoid scalding. Stir constantly during the heating process. Add milk to the roux.

3. Bring mixture to a boil. Season with salt. Remove from heat. Reserve for use with Creamed Spinach.

HOLLANDAISE SAUCE

- 3 egg yolks
- Dash of hot sauce
- 2 teaspoons of freshly squeezed lemon juice
- 6 ounces of melted butter
- 1/8 teaspoon of cayenne pepper
- 1/2 teaspoon of salt

1. In a small, non-reactive mixing bowl, whip the egg yolks briskly. Add the hot sauce and lemon juice.

2. Bring a small saucepot of water to a boil. Reduce to a simmer or until steam begins to rise from the pot. Place the bowl containing the egg yolk mixture over the steam and cook for one minute, whisking continuously.

3. Slowly whisk-in the butter. Add seasonings. Set aside.

To assemble:

- 1½ cups of Creamed Spinach (See recipe on facing page)
- 8 plain artichoke hearts
- 4 eggs, poached
- Hollandaise Sauce (See recipe above)

1. Place one-third cup of the hot Creamed Spinach in the center of four serving plates.

2. Top spinach with two artichoke hearts. Top artichokes with one poached egg. Top egg with Hollandaise Sauce. Serve hot.

Serves four.

– Antoine's Restaurant
French Quarter, New Orleans

Quiche Lorraine

Real men do indeed eat quiche around New Orleans. It's the brunch dish that refuses to die, mostly because of its wonderful flavor and ability to feed a crowd.

- 1 9-inch single pie crust, frozen
- 1/2 pound of bacon,
  cooked crispy and crumbled
- 1 cup of shredded Swiss cheese
- 1/3 cup of minced onion
- 4 eggs, beaten
- 2 cups of light cream
- 3/4 teaspoon of salt
- 1/4 teaspoon of white sugar
- 1/8 teaspoon of cayenne pepper

1. Preheat oven to 425 degrees.

2. Layer bacon, cheese and onion into pastry shell.

3. In a medium-sized mixing bowl, whisk together eggs, cream, salt, sugar and cayenne pepper. Pour mixture into pastry shell.

4. Bake 15 minutes in the preheated oven. Then, reduce heat to 300 degrees and bake an additional 30 minutes, or until a knife inserted one inch from the edge comes out clean.

5. Allow quiche to sit 10 minutes before serving.

Serves six.

– Elayne Angel
French Quarter, New Orleans

Calas

"Belle calas! Tout chaud!" *That's what the street vendors in the French Quarter used to singsong when their prize cakes were lovely, hot and crisp. You'd be hard-pressed to find such a street vendor nowadays, but this recipe still turns out calas that are lovely, hot and crisp.*

- ½ cup of leftover, cooked white rice
- 1 package of dry active yeast
- ½ cup of warm water
- 1¼ cups of all-purpose flour
- ½ cup of sugar
- 3 eggs, lightly beaten
- ¼ teaspoon of ground allspice
- Vegetable oil for frying
- Powdered sugar

1. Warm the rice and mash with a potato masher.

2. In a bowl, dissolve the yeast in one-half cup of warm water, stirring well; let sit until the yeast begins to bubble, five to ten minutes.

3. Add dissolved yeast to rice and stir well. Cover and let stand overnight at room temperature.

4. In a mixing bowl, combine flour, sugar, eggs and allspice. Add rice mixture. Cover and let rise in a warm place, free from drafts, for about 15 minutes.

5. Heat oil in a deep skillet, then gently drop tablespoon-sized dollops of the mixture into the hot oil. Cook for one minute, or until golden brown on all sides.

6. Drain well, sprinkle with powdered sugar, and serve warm.

Makes about two and a half dozen.

– Elizabeth's Restaurant
The Bywater District, New Orleans

French Bread

Few people in New Orleans bake their own French bread, since the loaves on sale are good and inexpensive. But if you wish to try your hand, here's a recipe that works well.

- 4 cups of all-purpose flour
- 1 package of dry yeast
- 1½ teaspoons of salt
- 1¾ cups of hot water (105-115 degrees)
- 2 tablespoons of vegetable oil
- Olive oil

1. In a large bowl, measure the flour and mix-in the dry yeast and salt.

2. Form a well in the center of the mixture, pour in the water and add the vegetable oil.

3. Using a wooden spoon, slowly combine the flour and water by gently pulling the flour into the liquid until it's fully absorbed.

4. Work the flour by hand until you can form a ball. Remove dough from the bowl and place on a floured work surface. The dough should be slightly tacky. If it is too sticky, add a bit of flour.

5. Knead the dough until it becomes elastic, for five or ten minutes.

6. Transfer the dough to a greased bowl and cover with a damp kitchen towel. Place in a warm place and allow the dough to rise. You can place it on top of your dryer and turn the dryer on low heat. The dough will double in size in about an hour and a half.

7. When the dough has risen fully, place it on a floured surface and work it to get rid of any air pockets. Divide dough in half and shape into large baguettes. Divide the dough into smaller baguettes for individual sandwiches.

8. Brush dough with olive oil and set in a warm place. The dough will rise again, so be sure to shape the loaves according to your desired size and the size of your oven. The dough will be finished rising in about 15 minutes.

9. Preheat your oven to 375 degrees.

10. Bake for 30 to 35 minutes, or until the crust is golden brown. Cool.

– Bryan Civello
Faubourg Marigny District
New Orleans

Corn Bread

There's nothing better than corn bread when you're eating red beans and rice — or any kind of beans and rice, for that matter. It's perfect, too, for sopping up the "pot liquor" from a pot of smothered greens.

- ½ cup of sifted all-purpose flour
- 1½ cups of yellow cornmeal
- 1 teaspoon of Creole seasoning
- 2 teaspoons of sugar
- 3 teaspoons of baking powder
- 3 eggs, lightly beaten
- 1 cup of milk
- ¼ cup of heavy cream
- ½ cup of melted butter

1. Preheat oven to 400 degrees.

2. Combine dry ingredients in a bowl, then add eggs and milk.

3. Beat with a spoon until moist, then thoroughly incorporate cream and butter.

4. Pour into a buttered pan and bake until set and golden brown, 15 to 20 minutes.

Statue of Louis "Satchmo" Armstrong, one of New Orleans' most famous and beloved musicians.

Shrimp Remoulade

In France, remoulade sauce is pretty bland, showing up at the table either white or green. In New Orleans it tends to be red and pungent, good on many things but world-class on our glorious Gulf shrimp.

- 1 bunch of celery, coarsley chopped
- 1 bunch of green onions, coarsley chopped
- 1 bunch of parsley, coarsley chopped
- 1 large yellow onion, coarsley chopped
- 1 cup of ketchup
- 1 cup of tomato puree
- 1 cup of Creole mustard
- 1 cup of red wine vinegar
- 2 tablespoons of prepared horseradish
- 2 teaspoons of Worcestershire sauce
- 1 cup of salad oil
- 1 ounce of paprika
- 4 pounds of jumbo boiled shrimp, peeled
- 1 head of lettuce

1. Place celery, green onions, parsley, and onion in a food processor and process until ingredients are thoroughly minced.

2. Add ketchup, tomato puree, Creole mustard, red wine vinegar, horseradish, Worcestershire sauce and oil to the vegetables. Mix these ingredients in the food processor until thoroughly combined. Add paprika last and pulse to incorporate.

3. Transfer mixture to a non-reactive bowl and refrigerate six to eight hours before serving.

4. Prior to serving, taste again and adjust horseradish if necessary.

5. In a large mixing bowl, toss the shrimp with the remoulade sauce, making sure to evenly coat the shrimp. Serve on beds of lettuce.

Serves 12.

– Galatoire's Restaurant
French Quarter, New Orleans

Crabmeat-Stuffed Avocado

Because of its vibrant port and its long association with Latin America, New Orleanians have had a love affair with avocadoes for many generations. The blending of the delicate tastes of avocado and crabmeat creates a dish fit for a king and queen.

- 12 ounces of crabmeat, picked over
  for shells and cartilage
- 8 ounces of cream cheese, softened
- 4 tablespoons of mayonnaise
- 1/3 cup of finely chopped iceberg lettuce
- 1/3 cup of drained and chopped black olives
- 1/4 teaspoon of garlic powder
- 3 avocados, halved and pitted
- 3/4 teaspoon of paprika
- 1/4 teaspoon of freshly ground black pepper

1. Gently combine the crabmeat with the cream cheese, mayonnaise, lettuce, olives and garlic powder.

2. Spoon the mixture into the avocado halves and sprinkle with paprika and pepper.

3. Refrigerate 30 minutes before serving.

Serves six.

Oysters *en Brochette*

Oysters and bacon are a marriage made in heaven, as any veteran of Japanese rumaki will attest. Here's an even better way to keep the marriage happy.

- 10 slices of bacon
- 36 raw oysters
- Flour seasoned with salt and pepper
- 2/3 cup of butter
- 1/3 cup of olive oil
- Toast points
- 1 teaspoon of lemon juice

1. Cut the bacon into one-inch pieces and fry in a skillet until partially cooked, draining off fat.

2. Alternate six oysters with six pieces of bacon on skewers.

3. Roll in seasoned flour, then sauté in the butter and olive oil just until golden brown. Turn meat to cook on all sides.

4. Transfer skewered meat to a platter lined with toast points.

5. Add lemon juice to the skillet and swirl into the butter and oil. Pour this sauce over the meat.

Serves six.

– Galatoire's Restaurant
French Quarter, New Orleans

Creole *Daube Glacé*

In traditional New Orleans households, daube glacé is daube lifted to the highest level imaginable. This famous dish, seen less and less often, is a molded and chilled presentation of a flavorful but less tender cut of meat that's been slowly braised with vegetables and spices.

- 2-pound beef roast
- 8 to 10 cloves of garlic, peeled
- Salt and cayenne pepper, to taste
- ½ cup of dry red wine
- 1 cup of beef stock
- 20 large green olives stuffed with pimiento, sliced
- 2 cups of beef broth
- 2 packages of unflavored gelatin
- 5 green onions, minced
- 2 tablespoons of minced parsley
- 1 tablespoon of Worcestershire sauce
- 1 teaspoon of Tabasco sauce

1. Rinse the roast, make slits throughout, stuff with garlic, and season with salt and pepper.

2. Place roast in a crock pot. Add the wine and beef stock. Cook on low for eight to ten hours.

3. Remove and cool. Shred one cup of the roast beef; set aside. (Reserve the remainder for po-boys.)

4. Layer green olives in a small mold or casserole dish. Sprinkle shredded beef over olives.

5. In a large bowl, prepare the gelatin using the beef broth – not water. Add the boiling beef broth to the gelatin until gelatin is completely dissolved.

6. Add remaining ingredients and mix thoroughly.

7. Chill until gelatin begins to gel. Pour gelatin slowly over the beef layer.

8. Chill until set, at least eight hours.

9. Gently unmold on a serving plate.

10. Serve chilled with crackers, or serve slices over a green salad.

Fried Green Tomatoes
with Crawfish Remoulade

Fried green tomatoes are, of course, a famed Southern dish from the countryside. Leave it to New Orleans restaurateurs to play around with topping fried green tomatoes with shrimp or crawfish remoulade.

- 4 green tomatoes, sliced in ¼-inch slices
- Salt and black pepper
- 1/4 cup of all-purpose flour
- 2 eggs, beaten
- 2 cups of cornmeal, for breading
- 1 cup of vegetable oil, heated in an iron skillet
- Crawfish Remoulade (Recipe follows)

1. Season tomato slices with salt and pepper.

2. Dust with flour.

3. Dip in beaten eggs and coat with cornmeal.

4. Fry in hot oil until browned, about three minutes on each side.

5. Serve three slices of fried tomatoes topped with Crawfish Remoulade.

CRAWFISH REMOULADE

- 1/2 stalk of celery, coarsely chopped
- 1/4 white onion, coarsely chopped
- 1/4 bellpepper, coarsely chopped
- 1 clove of garlic, peeled
- 1/4 teaspoon of Worcestershire sauce
- 2 tablespoons of Creole mustard
- 1 tablespoon of yellow mustard
- 2 teaspoons of ketchup
- Salt and black pepper, to taste
- 3 tablespoons of olive oil
- 1/8 teaspoon of cayenne
- Juice from 1/2 of a fresh lemon
- 1/2 pound of cooked peeled crawfish tails

1. Combine above ingredients, except crawfish tails, in a food processor. Process until smooth. Adjust seasoning.

2. Add crawfish tails and stir.

3. Cover and chill.

Serves eight.

– David Gordin
Faubourg Marigny District
New Orleans

Shrimp Cocktail

With such incredible shrimp through so many seasons of the year, it makes sense that each New Orleans cook has perfected his/her own version of cocktail sauce. The one contained in this recipe is so good that you can just eat it on crackers.

- ½ dill pickle, finely chopped
- 1 (14-ounce) bottle of ketchup
- 1 tablespoon of Tabasco
- ½ teaspoon of salt
- 1 teaspoon of Worcestershire sauce
- 1 tablespoon of mayonnaise
- 1 cup of finely chopped celery
- ½ green bellpepper, finely chopped
- Juice of 1 lemon
- ¼ teaspoon of sugar
- 1 teaspoon of prepared horseradish
- 5 cloves of garlic, minced
- 36 medium shrimp, boiled, peeled and chilled
- Shredded lettuce

1. Combine all ingredients except the shrimp and lettuce in a bowl. Refrigerate for at least 30 minutes.

2. Cover appetizer plates with a layer of shredded lettuce and serve six shrimp per person.

3. Cover with cocktail sauce.

Serves six.

FRENCH MARKET

Tomato Festival   FRENCH   MARKET   Welcomes Yucatan

For a couple of centuries, the French Market has been a great place to buy fresh produce and many other kinds of goods.

Vegetables & Salads

Creamed Spinach

Originally called Uncle Martin's Creamed Spinach, this dish was created by an uncle of Ruth Fertel's. The late Ms. Fertel is the founder of the nationally renowned Ruth's Chris Steakhouse chain. Next to steaks, this is one of the restaurant's most popular side dishes. It was introduced to the dining public at Ruth's Chris' original location, on Broad Street in New Orleans.

- ½ cup of flour
- 3 cups of half & half, divided
- 3 (10-ounce) packages of chopped frozen spinach, thawed and drained
- 1 cup of butter, chipped
- 1 tablespoon of salt
- 1½ teaspoons of ground black pepper

1. In a medium saucepot over medium heat, mix flour and one cup of half & half to make a paste, whisking until smooth.

2. Add spinach and blend well.

3. Add butter, two cups of half & half, salt and pepper to spinach mixture.

4. Cook mixture on low heat for 20 minutes or until desired consistency is reached.

Serves six to eight.

– Ruth's Chris Steakhouse
New Orleans and Metairie

Creole Green Beans

Taste these green beans and you'll never again hate the phrase, "Eat your vegetables." The onion helps things along, but it's the crumbled bacon and bacon drippings that tell the world these are special green beans.

- 2 cups of water
- 1 pound of fresh snap beans
- 6 tablespoons of bacon drippings
- 2 tablespoons of crumbled, crispy bacon
- 1 small onion, chopped
- ½ teaspoon of sugar
- Salt and black pepper, to taste

1. In a large saucepan, combine all the ingredients. Cover tightly and bring to a boil. Boil for five minutes.

2. Reduce heat and simmer for 15 minutes or until beans are cooked and water has evaporated.

3. Check seasonings and serve.

– Noel Rideout
Faubourg Marigny District
New Orleans

Creole White Beans

Sometimes New Orleanians like a change from the ever-popular red beans and rice: They love white beans, for instance. Most bean recipes have a lot in common with all other bean recipes. Happily, the beans themselves are different and bring a different spin on "soul food" to New Orleans dinner tables.

- ¼ cup of salad oil
- 1 pound of andouille sausage, sliced into "half moons"
- 1 large onion, diced
- 1 bellpepper, diced
- 2 tablespoons of minced garlic
- 1 tablespoon of basil
- 1 tablespoon of oregano
- 1 tablespoon of thyme
- 1 tablespoon of fresh cracked black pepper
- 2 tablespoons of salt
- 2 or 3 dashes of Tabasco
- 1 pinch of cayenne pepper
- 1 whole bay leaf
- 3 ounces of white wine
- ¼ cup of Worcestershire sauce
- 1 pound of dry white beans, soaked overnight
- 6 to 8 cups of water

1. In a large saucepot, heat oil over medium-high heat.

2. Sauté sausage, vegetables and spices for three to five minutes.

3. Deglaze by pouring in the white wine and Worcestershire and scraping the brown bits to dislodge them from the bottom of the pot.

4. Add beans and water and simmer for 45 to 60 minutes, or until beans are tender.

5. Season to taste, and serve over hot rice.

Serves six to eight.

Maque Choux

Though usually credited to the Cajuns, this wonderful smothered corn dish probably goes back to the Attakapas tribe, who taught the Cajuns quite a bit about living off the land.

- 24 ears of sweet corn
- 2 onions, finely chopped
- 2 large bellpeppers, chopped
- 4 over-sized tomatoes, or a 15-ounce can of whole tomatoes
- ½ pound of butter (2 sticks)
- 2 tablespoons of salt
- 2 tablespoons of black pepper

1. Cut corn off the cob; shave down the cob to get the juice. (Shave each cob right after cutting kernels from it; then move on to the next.)

2. Sauté onion, bellpepper and tomato in butter for about 10 minutes.

3. Add corn and cook until tender, about 15 minutes. (If corn takes longer to get soft, add some milk and a little more butter.)

4. Add salt and pepper about five minutes into cooking corn.

Serves eight to ten.

– Chef Alex Patout
Alex Patout's Louisiana Restaurant
French Quarter, New Orleans

Smothered Okra

- 1/3 cup of vegetable oil
- 2 pounds of okra, washed under cool water, stemmed and cut crosswise into 1/2-inch slices
- 3 cups of chopped onions
- 2 cups of chopped bellpeppers
- 1 cup of chopped celery
- 2 (1-pound) cans of whole tomatoes, crushed with their liquid
- 3 teaspoons of salt
- 1/2 teaspoon of cayenne
- 3/4 cup of water or chicken broth

1. Preheat the oven to 350 degrees.

2. Pour the oil into the bottom of a large roasting pot, not cast iron.

3. Add the remaining ingredients and stir to mix well. Cover the pot with a lid.

4. Bake, stirring occasionally, for 30 minutes, then reduce the heat to 300 degrees.

5. Continue baking, with the lid on, for one and a half to two hours, or until the slime has disappeared.

6. Bake uncovered for the last 15 minutes of the cooking time. The time will vary according to the tenderness of the okra.

7. Remove and cool completely before storing in freezer containers.

Note: This is excellent to serve as a side dish or to use as the base for okra gumbo.

Serves 10.

– Marcelle Bienvenu

Smothered Greens

Like anything smothered — especially greens — this dish is best prepared according to African-American tradition, with both bacon and ham hocks for flavor.

- 6 pounds of greens (turnip, mustard or mixed)
- ½ pound of lean bacon, cut into one-inch pieces
- 1 cup of chopped onion
- ½ cup of chopped celery
- ½ cup of chopped green bellpepper
- 2 pounds of ham hocks
- Salt, to taste
- Black pepper, to taste
- 2 cups of water
- Hot peppered vinegar, to taste

1. Break the greens into two-inch pieces; set aside.

2. Fry the bacon in a large skillet until rendered, then add the onion, celery and bellpepper. Cook about five minutes, and then add the greens.

3. Cover and cook until wilted, 12 to15 minutes.

4. Add the ham hocks. Season with salt and pepper.

5. Pour in the water and peppered vinegar, cover and simmer for one and one-half hours.

Serves eight to ten.

Fried Eggplant

Sicily left its fingerprints on this savory starter or snack. Be sure to have plenty of your favorite marinara sauce handy for dipping.

- 3 eggs
- 1½ cups of milk
- 2 large eggplants, peeled and cut into ¾-inch-thick strips
- 2 cups of all-purpose flour
- 4 cups of breadcrumbs
- Creole seasoning, to taste
- Oil for deep frying
- Marinara sauce

1. Combine the eggs and milk.

2. Dredge eggplant strips in flour, then dip in egg wash, then roll in breadcrumbs seasoned with Creole seasoning.

3. Deep-fry in batches until golden brown.

4. Drain on paper towels.

5. Serve with marinara sauce.

Serves six to eight.

Potatoes *au Gratin*

Butter, cream or milk, cheese — sounds like a promotion from the Dairy Board. And it also sounds like some of the ingredients for the perfect dish for New Orleans taste buds.

- 3 cups of diced cooked potatoes
- 6 tablespoons of butter
- 3 tablespoons of all-purpose flour
- 1½ cups of milk
- 1 cup of shredded cheddar cheese
- Salt and black pepper, to taste
- 1 cup of breadcrumbs

1. Preheat the oven to 400 degrees.

2. Arrange potatoes in a shallow ovenproof baking dish or casserole.

3. Melt the butter in a saucepan, then transfer about half of it to a bowl.

4. Stir the flour into the butter in the saucepan, then gradually stir-in the milk, until the sauce thickens.

5. Add the cheese and stir until it is melted; add seasonings.

6. Pour the sauce over the potatoes, mixing gently.

7. Combine the breadcrumbs with the butter in the bowl, then spread this mixture over the top of the potatoes.

8. Bake uncovered for about 15 minutes, then broil until top is golden brown.

Serves four.

Brabant Potatoes

From corner cafes to fine dining establishments, New Orleans chefs are known to push aside traditional french fries and hash browns for this delicate version of fried potatoes. The culinary roots of the brabant may trace back to traditional French cuisine, but served in New Orleans brabants add a bit of haute cuisine style when served with eggs, steak, fried fish or even burgers.

- 2 medium baking potatoes, peeled and cut into ½-inch cubes (about 1 pound)
- 2 tablespoons of vegetable oil
- ½ teaspoon of salt
- ¼ teaspoon of freshly ground black pepper
- ¼ cup of chopped green onions
- 2 tablespoons of chopped parsley
- 1 tablespoon of Worcestershire sauce
- 1 tablespoon of chopped garlic
- 2 tablespoons of butter

1. Put the potatoes in a saucepan and cover with water.

2. Boil for four to five minutes, or until slightly tender. Drain and cool slightly.

3. Heat the oil in a nonstick skillet over medium-high heat.

4. Add the potatoes, salt, and pepper.

5. Cook, shaking the pan back and forth, for 10 to 12 minutes, or until golden brown and crisp.

6. Add the green onions, parsley, Worcestershire, and garlic.

7. Shake the pan again for about one minute.

8. Add the butter and continue shaking the pan until it is melted. Serve immediately.

– Chef Emeril Lagasse
From *Louisiana Real & Rustic* Cookbook

Lyonnaise Potatoes

When we're not going au gratin, *we're heading for Lyon. That French gastronomic capital works wonders with something as simple as cubed potatoes.*

- 3 tablespoons of butter
- 1 large white onion, thinly sliced
- 1½ pounds of russet potatoes, boiled, peeled and cut into ¼-inch cubes
- Salt and freshly ground black pepper, to taste
- Chopped fresh parsley

1. Heat the butter in a large heavy skillet and sauté the onion until lightly browned.

2. Add the potatoes, salt and pepper and sauté until potatoes are golden, with a slightly crisp crust.

3. Garnish with chopped parsley.

Serves four to six.

Sweet Potatoes Royale

In Louisiana, the words "yam" and "sweet potato" are used interchangeably. In New Orleans and throughout the state, our favorite variety of sweet potato is officially known as the Louisiana yam.

- 1 large can of sweet potatoes
- 2/3 cup of sugar
- 2 eggs, beaten
- 1 stick of butter
- 1 teaspoon of cinnamon
- 2 tablespoons of all-purpose flour
- Topping (Recipe follows)

1. Preheat oven to 350 degrees.

2. Butter a large glass baking dish.

3. Mix together the sweet potatoes, sugar, eggs, butter, cinnamon and flour. Pour mixture in the baking dish.

4. Pour Topping over the top of the mixture.

5. Bake uncovered for 30 minutes.

TOPPING

- 1/2 stick of butter
- 4 teaspoons of all-purpose flour
- 2/3 cup of packed brown sugar
- 1½ cups of chopped pecans
- Pinch of cinnamon

1. Melt butter in a medium-size saucepan.

2. Add remaining ingredients and stir until fully incorporated.

Serves six.

Potato Salad

Many of us in New Orleans like our potato salad to tend toward the mustard-yellow, with just a little bit of a kick from the Creole seasoning.

- 3 pounds of red potatoes
- 2 hard-boiled eggs, chopped
- ½ cup of finely chopped celery
- 4 sprigs of parsley, finely chopped
- ½ green bellpepper, finely chopped
- ½ onion, finely chopped
- 3 tablespoons of yellow mustard
- ½ teaspoon of Creole seasoning

1. Peel and dice potatoes, then boil until just tender.

2. Drain and cool potatoes.

3. In a large bowl, combine potatoes with all remaining ingredients.

4. Refrigerate until ready to serve.

Serves eight to ten.

Fried Green Tomatoes

- 3 green tomatoes
- 1 cup of all-purpose flour
- Salt and black pepper, to taste
- 1 tablespoon of chopped basil
- 1 cup of seasoned Italian breadcrumbs
- 1 cup of milk
- 1 egg
- 1 cup of water
- Hot pepper sauce
- 1½ cups of vegetable oil

1. Slice tomatoes one-half-inch thick and drain on paper towels.

2. Season flour with salt and pepper.

3. Add chopped basil to the breadcrumbs.

4. Prepare egg wash by combining milk, egg and water. Blend well using a wire whisk. Season to taste using salt, pepper and hot pepper sauce.

5. Dredge tomato slices first in flour, next in egg wash and finally in breadcrumbs.

6. Fry a few at a time in 350-degree oil in a cast iron skillet until golden brown on each side. Remove and drain well.

7. Serve topped with a remoulade or tartar sauce.

Makes four servings of four tomato slices each.

– Chef John Folse

Crabmeat Salad

When the crabs are running — the local way of describing a great time indeed — you will be looking for ways to use up the sweet meat you pick from the shells, preferably surrounded by family and friends. Here's the tastiest crabmeat salad we've ever found.

- 1 teaspoon of Tabasco sauce
- 4 tablespoons of mayonnaise
- 1/3 cup of virgin olive oil
- 1/2 cup of small capers, drained
- 1 tablespoon of Dijon mustard
- 1/4 cup of lemon juice
- 1/2 teaspoon of black pepper
- 1/4 teaspoon of cayenne pepper
- 1 tablespoon of finely minced garlic
- 1 cup of finely chopped green onion
- 1/2 cup of finely chopped parsley
- 1/2 teaspoon of salt
- 1 pound of lump crabmeat, picked over for shells and cartilage
- 1 head of lettuce
- Slices of avocado, red onion and hearts of palm, for garnish (optional)

1. In a large mixing bowl, combine all ingredients except crabmeat, lettuce and optional garnishing items.

2. Delicately fold-in crabmeat so as not to break up the lumps.

3. Refrigerate for at least one hour prior to serving atop lettuce.

4. Garnish with salad options.

Makes four servings.

– Dawn DeDeaux
Faubourg Marigny District
New Orleans

Godchaux Salad

Several of the French Quarter's classic Creole palaces created salads over the years that diners will forever associate with their experiences there. The Godchaux salad is certain to conjure up Galatoire's to all who have stood in line at its Bourbon Street door over the decades.

- 1 head of iceberg lettuce, cleaned and cut into large ribbons
- 2 large tomatoes, cored and chopped
- 1 pound of jumbo lump crabmeat, picked over for shells and cartilage
- 30 large shrimp, boiled and peeled
- 2/3 cup of salad oil
- 1/3 cup of red wine vinegar
- 1/2 cup of Creole mustard
- 3 eggs, hard-boiled and chopped
- 12 anchovy filets

1. In a large salad bowl, combine the iceberg lettuce, tomatoes, crabmeat and shrimp.

2. In a small bowl, combine the oil, vinegar and Creole mustard, and whisk together to create the dressing.

3. Pour the dressing over the salad and toss.

4. Divide the salad onto six chilled plates.

5. Garnish each salad with chopped eggs and two anchovy filets.

Serves six.

– Galatoire's Restaurant
French Quarter, New Orleans

Creole Ambrosia

If you're looking for a simple dessert or refreshing summer salad, look no further than this tropical-tasting festival of local fruits.

- 2 cups of peeled and seeded satsuma sections
- 1 cup of peeled and chopped orange sections
- ½ cup of peeled and chopped ripe figs
- 2 large ripe bananas, sliced in ¼-inch slices
- 1 (12-ounce) can of fruit cocktail
- 1 (6-ounce) can of crushed pineapple
- 6 ounces of flaked coconut
- 2½ cups (20 ounces) of whipped topping (Cool Whip)

1. Combine above ingredients in a large glass bowl.

2. Stir gently to fully incorporate the juices and whipped topping without crushing the fruit.

3. Cover and chill for four hours.

4. Serve from the large bowl or scoop into individual dishes.

5. Garnish with cherries and extra whipped topping if you like.

Serves eight.

– Princess Ramona
Lower Garden District
New Orleans

St. Louis Cathedral and a statue of General Andrew Jackson
are two of the many historical features of Jackson Square.

The Multi-Ethnic Origins Of
GUMBO

Gumbo is perhaps the most famous of all south Louisiana foods. It is the best-known Creole and Cajun dish – and certainly one of the tastiest.

Webster's Dictionary defines gumbo as "a soup thickened with okra pods and usually containing vegetables with meat or seafoods." It's also defined as "a mixture or mélange."

The word "gumbo" stems from the African word for "okra" in several dialects. In the Belgian Congo the word for okra is "*tsingombo*;" in Angola, "*otsingombo*" and "*kingombo*." One theory holds that okra was introduced to the South by African slaves who brought it with them in their hair.

The evolution of gumbo into the dish we know today took a couple of centuries or more. Many people through many generations from several ethnic groups contributed to the development of this famous food, namely, Africans, Native American Indians, the French, the French-Acadians and the Spaniards.

Even in Louisiana's colonial period, gumbo was a popular dish because it was not only delicious but easy to prepare. Creole and Cajun women could tend to their duties in the house or in the field or garden while their gumbo simmered on the stove. It was also popular because of its flexibility and adaptability: The gumbo could be made with virtually anything that could be grown, gathered, raised, fished or hunted. Today, it is still a very practical – and satisfying – dish for the same reasons.   – From *The Louisiana Gumbo Cookbook*

Creole Onion Soup

Served in a traditional "tête de lion," or lion tureen, the classic French preparation is browned over the top, with a thick layer of cheese coating usually spilling over the sides of the bowl. The rich beef stock and onions create a wonderful soup. We've added Creole seasoning and left out the cheese to showcase the New Orleans-inspired variation.

- ½ cup of olive oil
- ½ cup of all-purpose flour
- 6 cups of julienne-sliced onion
- 2 cloves of garlic, minced
- 1½ teaspoons of salt
- 2 bay leaves
- 2 tablespoons of Creole seasoning
- ½ gallon of beef stock
- 8 slices of French bread, sliced thin and round to fit in the bottom of the serving bowl (Dry in the oven to crispy crouton consistency.)

1. Heat the oil in a large soup pot over medium-high heat. Slowly add the flour and stir constantly until you have created a smooth white roux, about four minutes.

2. Add the onion and sauté until translucent, about 10 minutes.

3. Add the garlic and continue to sauté until you smell the garlic cooking, about one minute.

4. Add the seasonings and stir to fully incorporate. Continue to cook for one minute.

5. Stir-in the beef stock, bring to a boil and reduce to a simmer. Simmer the soup for about 45 minutes to one hour.

6. Place the French bread on the bottom of the bowls, ladle soup on top and serve immediately.

7. You can garnish with minced onion or grated cheese.

Serves four to six.

Turtle Soup

Preparing Turtle Soup has reached the status of a culinary art form in New Orleans restaurants. And no one does it better than the chefs at Commander's Palace. They serve a hearty version of the soup, which makes a meal all by itself.

- 12 tablespoons (1½ sticks) of butter, divided
- 2½ pounds of turtle meat diced into ¾" pieces
- Kosher salt and freshly ground black pepper, to taste
- 2 medium onions, diced
- 6 stalks of celery, diced
- 1 large head of garlic, cloves peeled and minced
- 3 bellpeppers, diced
- 1 tablespoon of ground dried thyme
- 1 tablespoon of ground dried oregano
- 4 bay leaves
- 2 quarts of veal stock or beef stock
- 1 cup of all-purpose flour
- 1 bottle (750 ml) of dry sherry
- 1 tablespoon of Tabasco sauce
- ¼ cup of Worcestershire sauce
- 2 large lemons, juiced
- 3 cups of tomatoes, peeled, seeded, and coarsely chopped
- 10 ounces of fresh spinach, washed thoroughly, stems removed, coarsely chopped
- 6 medium eggs, hard-boiled and chopped into large pieces

1. Melt four tablespoons of the butter in a large soup pot over medium to high heat.

2. Brown the meat in the hot butter, season with salt and pepper, and cook for about 18 to 20 minutes, or until liquid is nearly evaporated.

3. Add the onions, celery, garlic, and peppers, stirring constantly,

then add the thyme, oregano, and bay leaves. Sauté for 20 to 25 minutes, until the vegetables have caramelized.

4. Add the stock, bring to a boil, lower the heat, and simmer uncovered for 30 minutes, periodically skimming away any fat that comes to the top.

5. While the stock is simmering, make a roux in a separate pot. Melt the remaining eight tablespoons of butter over medium heat in a small saucepan and add the flour a little at a time, stirring constantly with a wooden spoon. Be careful not to burn the roux. After all the flour has been added, cook for about three minutes, until the roux smells nutty, is pale in color, and has the consistency of wet sand. Set aside until the soup is ready.

6. Using a whisk, vigorously stir the roux into the soup, a little at a time to prevent lumping.

7. Simmer for 25 minutes. Stir to prevent sticking on the bottom.

8. Add the sherry and bring to a boil. Add the hot sauce and the Worcestershire and simmer, skimming any fat or foam that comes to the top.

9. Add the lemon juice and tomatoes and return to a simmer.

10. Add the spinach and the chopped egg, bring to a simmer, and adjust salt and pepper before serving.

Note: We use alligator snapping turtles, a farm-raised, freshwater species available all year. Turtle meat usually comes in two-and-a-half pound portions, so this recipe is written to use that quantity. This turtle meat freezes well and can be ordered by mail. The soup freezes well, too.

Makes six quarts.

– Commander's Palace
New Orleans

Oyster & Artichoke Soup

The late Warren LeRuth, the city's finest food chemist and one of its greatest chefs, both created and popularized this now-common soup. It is uncommonly good and is found today on the menus of many of the city's fine restaurants.

- 2 large artichokes
- 15 oysters, with their liquor
- 2 bay leaves
- 2 tablespoons of unsalted butter
- 1 cup of chopped green onion
- 1 tablespoon of minced garlic
- 2 tablespoons of all-purpose flour
- 4 tablespoons of ground thyme
- 1 teaspoon of salt
- Ground white pepper, to taste
- 2 tablespoons of lemon juice
- Chopped fresh parsley

1. Set the artichokes in a pan and add water just to cover.

2. Bring to a boil and cook until tender, about 30 minutes, then remove from the water and let cool.

3. Peel off the tough outer leaves. Remove and slice the tender hearts and bottoms. Set aside.

4. Bring five cups of water to a boil in a soup pot. Add the oysters with their liquor and the bay leaves. Simmer for about 10 minutes.

5. In a separate pot, melt the butter and sauté the green onion about three minutes, then add the minced garlic and flour, blending thoroughly.

6. Add this mixture to the simmering oysters and stock, stirring over medium heat until the soup thickens.

7. Take three oysters from the soup, dice them and return them to the soup.

8. Add the sliced artichokes.

9. Season with thyme, salt and white pepper. Add the lemon juice.

10. Add fresh parsley and simmer 10 more minutes before serving.

Serves six.

– Chef Warren LeRuth
New Orleans

Gumbo Ya-Ya
(Chicken & Sausage Gumbo)

Creoles and Cajuns have loved gumbo for as far back as anybody can remember.
Here's a version known in Creole patois as Gumbo Ya-Ya.

- 3 pounds of chicken wings
- 3 pounds of chicken thighs
- 2 pounds of bulk hot sausage
- 2 pounds of bulk pork sausage
- 1 tablespoon of butter or margarine
- 2 medium onions, chopped
- 2 stalks of celery, chopped
- 1 tablespoon of garlic powder
- 1 bellpepper, chopped
- 2 tablespoons of flour, dissolved in ½ cup
  of water (Mix thoroughly to dissolve any lumps.)
- 1 bay leaf
- 2 cups of chicken broth
- ½ gallon of water (adjust amount as needed)
- Salt and black pepper, to taste
- Cooked white rice
- Filé powder

1. The day before you want to serve the gumbo, boil chicken wings and thighs in a large soup pot until cooked, about 25 minutes. Use just enough water to cover chicken.

2. Cool and remove chicken meat from bones.

3. Return meat to the stock, cover and refrigerate overnight.

4. Remove pot with chicken stock from refrigerator and place on stove on medium-high heat.

5. In a large skillet, fry the sausage until cooked, about 20 minutes. Remove from heat and strain to get rid of excess grease.

6. Add cooked sausage to chicken stock.

7. In the same skillet, melt butter over medium-high heat. Sauté chopped onions, celery, garlic powder, and bellpepper. After onions are transparent and celery is cooked, five to seven minutes, add flour and bring to a boil.

8. Transfer this mixture to soup pot. Add bay leaf.

9. Add two cans of chicken broth plus water to soup pot. Season with salt and pepper. Bring to a boil, reduce to a simmer and cook for 45 minutes to an hour.

10. Serve in bowls over rice. Add a dash of filé to each bowl before serving.

Makes 10 to 12 servings.

– Cheryl Lemoine
Martin Wine Cellar
Metairie & Uptown New Orleans

Shrimp & Okra Gumbo

Shrimp & Okra Gumbo is one of the most delicious, most popular dishes ever created for a cold winter day in south Louisiana.

- Salt, black pepper and cayenne pepper, to taste
- 2 pounds of shrimp, peeled, deveined and cut in halves
- 2½ pounds of okra, cut in ½-inch pieces
- 6 tablespoons of vegetable oil
- 1 tomato, peeled and chopped fine
- 2 medium onions, chopped fine
- 2 celery ribs, sliced thin
- ¼ cup of bellpepper, chopped fine
- 1 can of Ro-Tel tomatoes
- 3 cloves of garlic, minced
- 1 tablespoon of tomato paste
- 6 green onions, minced
- 1 bay leaf
- 2 chicken bouillon cubes
- 1 teaspoon of white vinegar
- 3 quarts of water
- 1 bottle of clam juice
- 1 teaspoon of paprika
- 3 dashes of Tabasco sauce
- 1 tablespoon of Worcestershire
- 1 tablespoon of French's mustard
- ¼ cup of chopped green onion tops
- ¼ cup of fresh, chopped parsley
- 1 tablespoon of Kitchen Bouquet
- Hot cooked rice
- Filé

1. In a bowl, combine salt, black pepper and cayenne pepper. Dredge the shrimp in this seasoning. Set the shrimp aside.

2. Sauté the okra in the oil for half an hour. Add the chopped tomato, onion, celery, bellpepper, Ro-Tel tomatoes, garlic, tomato paste, green onions, bay leaf, bouillon cubes and white vinegar. Simmer for 30 more minutes.

3. Add the water and clam juice. Season with salt, black pepper and cayenne pepper. Add one teaspoon of paprika, Tabasco, Worcestershire and mustard. Cook for 30 minutes.

4. Add shrimp. Cook 30 minutes on medium heat. Remove bay leaf and discard.

5. Add green onion tops and parsley. Cook five minutes. Adjust seasonings.

6. Darken gumbo with Kitchen Bouquet, if desired.

7. To serve, mound rice in gumbo bowls, ladle some gumbo over the rice, and garnish with parsley.

8. Offer filé at the table.

– Bea Weber
Reprinted from *The Louisiana GUMBO Cookbook*

Gumbo Z'herbes

Gumbo is more Cajun than Creole, but like so many other famous dishes, New Orleanians certainly "Creolized" their own versions of gumbo. One in particular, gumbo z'herbes, is unrivaled when prepared by Leah Chase of Dooky Chase Restaurant. She's often called the "Queen of Creole Cuisine." She makes her version of gumbo z'herbes on Good Friday, the Friday before the Easter celebration. As with all Lenten dishes, you find no meat in this one. What you will find are plenty of greens. Each variety of greens in the dish is supposed to represent a new friendship to be formed in the coming year.

- 10 cups of water
- 5 cups of coarsely chopped spinach
- 5 cups of coarsely chopped mustard greens
- 5 cups of coarsely chopped beet greens
- 3 cups of coarsely chopped carrot tops
- 3 cups of coarsely chopped cabbage
- 2 cups of coarsely chopped watercress
- 2 cups of coarsely chopped radish tops
- 1/2 cup of coarsely chopped parsley
- 2 green onions, cut into 2-inch pieces
- 1 bay leaf
- 3 tablespoons of vegetable oil
- 2 stalks of celery, chopped
- 1 green bellpepper, chopped
- 1 cup of chopped onion
- 2 cloves of garlic, minced
- 1/4 cup of Tabasco sauce
- 1 tablespoon of salt
- 1 teaspoon of dried basil leaves
- 1 teaspoon of dried thyme leaves
- 1/8 teaspoon of ground allspice
- 3 tablespoons of butter or margarine (optional)
- 1/4 cup of all-purpose flour (optional)

1. In a large stock pot, place 10 cups of water, the greens, green onion and bay leaf, and bring to a boil. Reduce to a simmer and cook for 20 minutes or until all the greens are tender.

2. In a large skillet, heat oil over medium-high heat. Sauté celery, bellpepper, onion and garlic until softened, about 10 minutes.

3. Add hot sauce, salt, basil, thyme and allspice. Continue to cook for about two minutes.

4. Remove two cups of this vegetable mixture and place in the gumbo pot.

5. Process the remaining cooked vegetables in a blender for about 10 seconds. Transfer this mixture to the greens.

6. Continue to simmer the gumbo for another 20 minutes. Taste and adjust seasoning.

7. At this point you can use the butter and flour to make a roux to thicken the gumbo if you choose. (To make the roux, melt butter over medium heat in a medium-size skillet. Then stir-in flour and work out any lumps. Continue to cook, stirring constantly until the roux begins to turn a light brown. Remove it from the heat.)

8. Slowly whisk the roux into the gumbo until the desired thickness is reached. Cook the gumbo for an additional 10 to 12 minutes to make sure the flour flavor cooks out.

Crab & Corn Bisque

A classic bisque is created with cream and a puree of seafood, or in some cases, game. The spices, the cream and the puree technique make this style of soup rich and velvety.

- 2 tablespoons of olive oil
- 2 medium-size onions, finely chopped
- ¼ of a large bellpepper, chopped
- 2 ribs of celery, finely chopped
- 1 teaspoon of salt
- 1 teaspoon of freshly ground black pepper
- 1 teaspoon of dried sweet basil
- 3 bay leaves
- ½ teaspoon of dried thyme leaves
- 2 cloves of fresh garlic, peeled and minced
- 1 teaspoon of liquid crab boil
- 1 cup of chopped fresh mushrooms
- 1 16-ounce can of Italian-style tomatoes, coarsely diced
- 1 teaspoon of sugar
- 1 10-ounce can of cream of mushroom soup
- 1 16-ounce can of cream-style corn
- 2½ cups of fresh or canned whole-kernel corn, divided
- 1 pound of lump crabmeat, picked free of shells and divided
- 1 cup of half-and-half
- 2 tablespoons of fresh chopped parsley
- ½ pound of mild cheddar cheese, grated fine
- Salt and pepper, to taste
- Thinly sliced green onion tops

1. Heat oil to medium heat in a large soup pot.

2. Add onions and sauté until transparent, about three minutes.

3. Add bellpepper and celery and continue to sauté until vegetables are soft, about five minutes.

4. Add salt, pepper, sweet basil, bay leaves, thyme, garlic and liquid crab boil. Mix thoroughly and continue to sauté until you smell the garlic, about two minutes.

5. Add mushrooms, tomatoes and sugar. Bring to a boil, reduce to a simmer and continue to simmer for five to seven minutes.

6. Add mushroom soup, cream-style corn, one cup of the corn kernels and one-third of the crabmeat. Mix well.

7. Lower heat and continue to simmer for about 15 minutes to allow the flavors to come together.

8. Remove pot from heat and allow to cool for about 10 minutes.

9. Puree mixture with a stick blender – or transfer the liquid to a blender. Puree completely so there are no visible chunks of vegetables or spices.

10. Return pureed liquid to stove on low heat. Slowly add half-and-half, parsley and cheese.

11. Stir until cheese is completely melted and soup has taken on a rich texture.

12. Add remaining crabmeat and corn and continue to simmer on low heat for five to ten minutes.

13. Taste soup and adjust seasoning.

14. Serve in bowls and garnish with chopped green onions. Serve with French bread or crackers.

Serves six to eight.

Crawfish Bisque

Talk about your labor of love! The key to real crawfish bisque, as opposed to one or more versions of crawfish stew or etouffee, is spending the time stuffing the heads with a savory mix of tail meat and seasoned breadcrumbs. Many people prepare this bisque over two days.

DAY 1

- 20 pounds of live crawfish
- 4 packets of Zatarain's Crab, Shrimp and Crawfish Boil seasoning
- 3 whole lemons, quartered
- 50 pounds of ice (use 10-pound bags for easier handling)

1. Prepare a large crawfish-boiling pot with enough water for boiling the crawfish. You'll want to do this outside.

2. Add the crawfish seasoning and lemons to the boiling water. Carefully add the live crawfish to the boiling seasoned water and boil for 10 minutes. Once the crawfish are cooked, turn off the heat and let stand for five minutes. Carefully add most of the ice to cool the water. Let the crawfish soak in the seasoned water. The longer they soak the more flavor they will pick up.

3. Once the crawfish are thoroughly cooled, clean them as follows. Break off the tails. Reserve the "heads" in a clean pan. To peel the tails, simply remove the tail shell. Discard the "vein" but leave the meat flap in place. Discard tail shells. Place tail meat in a pan sitting on ice.

4. To clean the "heads," first remove the yellow fat globs and reserve them. (This is very important, as the "fat" adds lots of flavor to the dish. You need only about four or five dozen "heads" cleaned for stuffing, but you want all the "fat" from every "head.") After reserving the "fat," remove everything else in the "heads" and discard it.

70

Prepare the Stuffed Crawfish "Heads" according to the recipe below. (This is very labor-intensive, and it takes a long time. Most folks I know take two days to make crawfish bisque, cooking the crawfish, cleaning the "heads" and stuffing them on the first day, and cooking the bisque on the second day. Recruit some help if you can.)

STUFFED CRAWFISH "HEADS"

- ¼ cup of vegetable oil
- ½ cup of all-purpose flour
- 2 medium onions, finely minced
- 1 large bellpepper, finely minced
- Crawfish tail meat, divided
- Crawfish "fat," divided
- ¾ cup of seafood stock
- 2 teaspoons of salt
- Freshly ground black pepper
- 1½ teaspoons of cayenne pepper
- 2 large eggs, well beaten
- 2 cups of plain French breadcrumbs
- ¼ cup of chopped parsley
- ¼ cup of minced green onion tops
- 4 tablespoons of butter, melted
- 60 or so cleaned crawfish "heads"
- Flour for dusting

1. Make a medium-brown roux with the oil and flour over medium-high heat.

2. Add onions and bellpepper and cook until tender, stirring constantly, about 20 minutes.

3. Mince or grind half of the tail meat and add it to the roux. Add half of the crawfish "fat" and simmer for 15 to 20 minutes. (Refrigerate the remaining half of crawfish tail meat and crawfish "fat" for use on Day 2.)

(Continued on next page)

4. Add seafood stock, salt, peppers, eggs, breadcrumbs, parsley, green onions and butter. Combine thoroughly, adjusting the consistency with more stock or more breadcrumbs as needed. You want a mixture that is not too dry and not too wet.

5. Fill each "head" with stuffing. Roll "heads" in flour, making sure to flour the ends. Place "heads" on a baking sheet and bake at 350 degrees for 15 minutes. (You can fry the "heads" in vegetable oil, too. It takes about five minutes to cook them this way.)

6. Remove from oven, cool and refrigerate overnight.

DAY 2

TO MAKE THE BISQUE

- 6 tablespoons of butter
- ½ cup of vegetable oil
- 1 cup of all-purpose flour
- 2 large onions, finely minced
- 1 large bellpepper, finely minced
- 4 ribs of celery, finely minced
- 4 cloves of garlic, finely minced
- 5 cups of shellfish stock
- Crawfish tail meat reserved in refrigerator from Day 1
- Crawfish "fat" reserved in refrigerator from Day 1
- 1 tablespoon of Creole seasoning
- 1 tablespoon of salt
- 1 tablespoon of freshly ground black pepper
- 2 teaspoons of cayenne pepper (optional)
- 2 teaspoons of ground thyme
- 5 dozen Stuffed Crawfish "Heads"
- ½ cup of chopped green onion tops
- ½ cup of chopped parsley
- 8 cups of cooked long-grain white rice

1. In a large skillet, make a roux by heating the butter and oil over medium-high heat and slowly adding the flour and stirring until you have a wet sand consistency. Cook over low heat, stirring constantly until the mixture turns light brown.

2. Add the onions, bellpepper, celery and garlic, and continue to cook, stirring constantly, until the vegetables are soft. Remove from heat and cool, continuing to stir.

3. Gradually and carefully add the shellfish stock and combine thoroughly, making a nice gravy. Add the remaining half of the crawfish tails and crawfish "fat," Creole seasoning, salt and peppers, and thyme and cook over low heat for 20 to 25 minutes.

4. Using a stick blender, puree the bisque until smooth. Be careful not to burn yourself. (If you are uncomfortable with this step you can leave it out. It just makes a more aesthetically pleasing soup if it is silky smooth!)

5. Add the Stuffed "Heads" and cook over low heat for 20 minutes. When stirring be careful not to break open the "heads."

6. A few minutes before serving, add onion tops and parsley.

7. To serve, place about three-fourths cup of cooked rice in each bowl. Top with bisque and serve six heads per bowl.

Serves ten.

– Todd Duke
Mid-City, New Orleans

Bouillabaisse

New Orleans is a French city in so many ways. Therefore, while our ancestors here were busy rethinking almost every European dish into dishes like gumbo and jambalaya, they were also enjoying the original inspirations. This classic French bouillabaisse *shows just how far we've traveled from Marseilles — and why it's so nice to go back for a visit.*

- Fish Stock (Recipe follows)
- 1 onion, diced
- 1 leek, diced and cleaned (Use both the green and white parts.)
- 1 cup of diced celery
- 10 ounces of diced tomato
- 2 teaspoons of saffron
- 1 ounce of Pernod
- 4 ounces of diced fennel
- 2 ounces of snapper, diced
- 2 ounces of tuna, diced
- 3 ounces of shrimp, peeled and diced
- 4 ounces of mussels, diced
- 3 ounces of monkfish, diced
- Garlic Croutons (Recipe follows)
- Rouille (Recipe follows)

1. Place all of the vegetables, seasonings and seafood in a large pot containing the Fish Stock.

2. Simmer for eight minutes or until fish is cooked.

3. Adjust seasoning.

4. To assemble the dish, place about 12 ounces of the bouillabaisse in a large bowl.

5. Top with freshly baked Garlic Croutons.

6. Serve a tablespoon of Rouille on the side. Rouille is usually mixed with the hot bouillabaisse for extra flavor.

FISH STOCK

- 2 pounds of fish bones
- 1 quart of water
- 1 quart of dry white wine
- 1 carrot, peeled and diced
- 1 onion, peeled and diced
- 1 leek, cleaned and diced
- 1 cup of diced celery
- 2 bay leaves
- 8 black peppercorns

1. Combine all ingredients and bring to a boil in a large stockpot over high heat.

2. Reduce heat and simmer for 20 minutes.

3. Strain stock. Discard vegetables and bones. Reserve liquid.

GARLIC CROUTONS

- 1 large loaf of French bread, cut in one-inch pieces
- 2 ounces of garlic butter
- 1 tablespoon of grated Parmesan cheese

1. Preheat oven to 350 degrees.

2. Arrange pieces of bread on a baking sheet.

(Continued on next page)

3. Brush each piece of bread with garlic butter and sprinkle with Parmesan cheese.

4. Bake for about five minutes or until bread begins to turn golden brown.

ROUILLE

- 3 ounces of olive oil
- 1 ounce of garlic puree
- 2 ounces of sun-dried tomato
- Tabasco, to taste
- 1 egg
- 1 tablespoon of Dijon mustard

1. Combine all ingredients in a blender and blend until smooth.

2. Season to taste.

Serves four.

– René Bajeux
René Bistrot
Central Business District, New Orleans

New Orleans streetcars carry passengers by the thousands each day.

How The
Po-Boy
Came To Be

B ack in 1922, two brothers, Bennie and Clovis Martin, who'd
worked for a time as streetcar conductors in New Orleans,
opened a small sandwich shop in the French Quarter. A strike
between their old Streetcar Union and the City prompted the brothers to feed free of charge any unemployed union man who entered
their shop. The strike lasted for months.

When a member of the union would show up, the cry, "Here
comes another poor boy!" would be heard. New Orleanians eventually condensed the words to "po-boy."

The po-boy was originally made with 32-inch French loaves from
Gendusa Bakery, a business which is still in operation today.

By the way, the Martin brothers were a couple of Cajun guys
from Raceland, La. Their original New Orleans sandwich shop
was across from the French Market, at the corner of Ursuline and
North Peters; it moved in 1931 to a new location on the corner of
Touro and St. Claude.

Meatball Po-boy

The Sicilian immigrations changed New Orleans food forever. And even though most Sicilian contributions are now an uncredited part of Creole cooking, a few items manage to glisten and glow. There's no such thing as too often when it comes to a great meatball po-boy.

- 2 medium onions, peeled and finely chopped
- 2 bunches of green onions, finely chopped
- 2 cloves of garlic, peeled and finely chopped
- ½ cup of finely chopped fresh Italian parsley leaves
- 1½ cups of finely chopped fresh basil leaves
- 3 eggs, beaten
- 1 cup of unseasoned breadcrumbs
- 1¾ cups of water
- ¾ pounds of grated Romano cheese
- 4 tablespoons of salt
- 1 teaspoon of freshly ground black pepper
- 3½ pounds of ground beef
- 3½ pounds of ground pork
- All-purpose flour
- Olive oil
- French bread
- Marinara sauce

1. Combine the onion, green onion, garlic, parsley and basil with the eggs in a large bowl.

2. Add the breadcrumbs, water, cheese, salt and pepper.

3. Add the meats and mix well.

4. Roll the meat mixture into two-inch balls, using warm water to keep your hands moist.

5. Roll each meatball in flour and cook thoroughly in olive oil in a large skillet. Drain on paper towels.

6. Cut meatballs in half, arrange on sliced French bread, top with the marinara sauce of your choice, then cover with the remaining half of the French bread.

Roast Beef Po-Boy

Don't wear your good clothes when you settle in to eat a roast beef po-boy in New Orleans. The whole idea is that the French bread soaks up plenty of wonderful beef gravy.

- 4-pound beef roast
- 8 cloves of garlic, peeled and left whole
- Salt and black pepper, to taste
- 2 large onions, sliced
- 1 stalk of celery, chopped
- ½ cup of red wine
- 1 tablespoon of all-purpose flour
- 1 cup of water

1. Rinse the roast in cold water and pat it dry.

2. Make slits throughout the roast and stuff it with whole garlic cloves.

3. Season the roast with salt and pepper.

4. Place it in a crock pot with the sliced onion, celery, red wine and flour.

5. Add a cup of water.

6. Cover and cook on low setting for 10 to 12 hours. (The longer you cook the roast the more tender the beef becomes.) Check periodically and add water if necessary.

To assemble the sandwich:

- 1 small French bread loaf (12-inch),
  split in half lengthwise
- 1 tablespoon of mayonnaise
- ½ cup of iceberg lettuce, shredded
- 8 ounces of thinly sliced roast beef
- ¼ cup of thick beef gravy
- 1 small tomato, sliced thin

1. Warm the French bread in a hot oven for about two minutes.

2. Spread the mayonnaise on top and bottom layers of bread.

3. Add the lettuce, beef, gravy and tomato slices.

4. Close the bread and serve warm – with lots of napkins!

Serves two.

– Bryan Civello
Faubourg Marigny District
New Orleans

Muffaletta

Local history argues persuasively that the Tusa family created this Sicilian mega-sandwich near the start of the 20th century. It is said to have started out just for the poor Sicilian laborers of the French Market.

- 1 cup of green olives stuffed with pimientos, chopped
- ¾ cup of black olives in oil, chopped
- ½ cup of olive oil
- 1 tablespoon of chopped fresh oregano
- 6 tablespoons of chopped fresh Italian parsley
- Salt and pepper, to taste
- 2 teaspoons of minced garlic
- 1 teaspoon of fresh lemon juice
- 1 loaf of round Italian bread
- 1 medium Creole tomato, thinly sliced
- ¼ head of iceberg lettuce, shredded
- ¼ pound of Mortadella (sweet salami)
- ¼ pound of local New Orleans Chesesi ham or regular ham
- ¼ pound of Capicola
- ¼ pound of sliced mozzarella
- ¼ pound of thinly sliced pepperoni

1. In a large non-reactive mixing bowl, combine olives, oil, seasonings, garlic and lemon juice.

2. Cover and marinate overnight in refrigerator.

3. Cut Italian loaf in half horizontally and hollow-out the bottom layer for filling.

4. Remove the salad from the refrigerator and drain.

5. Divide the salad in half and place one-half on the hollowed-out slice of bread.

6. Layer with lettuce, tomato, and the meats and cheese as listed.

7. Top with the other half of the salad and place bread on top.

8. Wrap in plastic wrap tightly and place on baking sheet.

9. Top with a pan and weigh down with heavy weight – cans of food, phone book, etc.

10. Refrigerate for a few hours. Flavors will meld and the sandwich will be easier to slice.

11. Cut in small pieces and serve.

Serves two to four.

– Karen Stone
Upper Garden District
New Orleans

Red Beans & Rice

There is no food more New Orleans than red beans and rice. Just ask New Orleans' own Louis Armstrong, even if you have to find him in heaven. Maybe he's still signing his divine correspondence the way he signed just about everything during his lifetime: "Red beans and ricely yours!"

- 2 pounds of dried red kidney beans
- 2 cups of chopped onion
- ½ cup of chopped green onion tops
- ½ cup of chopped bellpepper
- 2 tablespoons of minced garlic
- 2 tablespoons of minced fresh parsley
- 1 tablespoon of salt
- ½ teaspoon of black pepper
- Pinch of cayenne pepper
- Pinch of crushed red pepper pods
- 2 whole bay leaves, broken in half
- ½ teaspoon of dried thyme
- ½ teaspoon of dried basil
- 3 to 4 quarts of water
- 1 pound of baked ham, cubed
- 1 or 2 ham hocks or ham bones
- Rice (See recipe on page 8)

1. Put all ingredients, except rice and ham, into a 10-quart pot.

2. Bring to a boil, then lower heat to simmer and cook for three to four hours or until beans are tender and a thick, natural gravy has formed.

3. Add the baked ham and ham hocks after the beans have been cooking for about two hours.

4. Serve over rice.

Note: If beans appear too dry, add more water. Stir the beans frequently during cooking to prevent scorching. If beans do not thicken by themselves, take a cup of the beans and mash them with a fork, then return mashed beans to the pot and simmer for 15 to 20 minutes.

Serving tip: Accompany with corn bread or French bread and a garden salad.

Serves 10 to 12.

Jambalaya

Jambalaya has got to be the best dish ever created to use up everything in your refrigerator. Here's a classic rendition with phenomenal flavors, but again don't feel too locked in. It isn't real jambalaya if you feel forbidden to put in just about anything you want.

- 2 tablespoons of vegetable oil
- 2 medium onions, chopped
- 4 green onions, chopped
- 2 stalks of celery, chopped
- 1 large bellpepper, chopped
- 3 garlic cloves, minced
- 2 teaspoons of salt
- 1 pound of andouille or smoked sausage, cut into ¾-inch-thick rounds
- 1 (15-ounce) can of whole peeled tomatoes in juice
- 2 tablespoons of Worcestershire
- 2 teaspoons of Creole seasoning
- 1/8 teaspoon of cayenne pepper (optional)
- 4 cups of water or chicken stock
- 2 cups of uncooked long-grain rice
- 1 pound of medium-size shrimp, cooked, peeled and deveined
- 2 tablespoons of chopped fresh parsley, for garnish

1. In a large stockpot, heat two tablespoons of vegetable oil.

2. Sauté the onions, celery and bellpepper for five to seven minutes.

3. Add garlic, salt and sausage and continue to sauté until sausage is browned, about five minutes.

4. Add tomatoes, Worcestershire, Creole seasoning and cayenne. Stir to incorporate seasonings and break up tomatoes.

5. Add water and rice and stir. Bring mixture to a boil and reduce to a simmer. Cover and cook until the rice has absorbed all the liquid, about 25 minutes.

6. Stir-in the shrimp and cover to heat, approximately five minutes.

7. Adjust seasonings, sprinkle with parsley and serve.

Serves six to eight.

– Emma Urban
Dauphine Street
New Orleans

Stuffed Peppers

The Indians of Louisiana were instrumental in helping to develop the cuisines of the Cajuns and Creoles. Corn, squash, beans and cornmeal were part of their daily repertoire and quickly found their way into the black iron pots. Here, we combine the Native American ingredients with beef to create an entree that's out of this world!

- ½ cup of butter
- 8 pounds of ground beef
- 2 cups of chopped onion
- 2 cups of chopped celery
- ½ cup of diced red bellpepper
- ½ cup of diced yellow bellpepper
- ½ cup of diced garlic
- 2 cups of beef stock
- 1 cup of sliced green onions
- ½ cup of chopped parsley
- 2 cups of whole-kernel corn
- 4 cups of crushed corn bread
- Salt and cracked black pepper, to taste
- Hot pepper sauce, to taste
- 4 each red, green and yellow bellpeppers
- 8 cups of prepared tomato sauce

1. In a large black iron skillet, melt butter over medium-high heat.

2. Add beef and cook until golden brown, approximately 30 minutes. Drain off all but two tablespoons of oil.

3. Add onions, celery, diced bellpeppers and garlic. Sauté three to five minutes or until vegetables are wilted.

4. Add beef stock to keep mixture moist while meat is sautéing.

5. Once tender, add green onions, parsley and corn.

6. Sprinkle-in crushed corn bread and blend well into meat mixture.

7. Season to taste using salt, pepper and hot sauce.

8. Cut off the tops of the bellpeppers and clean all pulp from the inside.

9. Stuff bellpeppers with the meat dressing, place them in a large casserole dish and surround them with prepared tomato sauce.

10. Bake in 375-degree oven for 30 minutes or until peppers are tender.

Serves 12.

– Chef John Folse

Stuffed Mirlitons

Mirlitons were made to be stuffed with seafood or meat. At least that's the sort of theology and logic you hear around New Orleans.

- 4 large mirlitons
- 1/2 stick of butter
- 1 medium onion, chopped
- 1/2 bellpepper, chopped
- 1 clove of garlic, minced
- 1 pound of ground beef
  (or you can substitute shrimp)
- 1 cup of Italian breadcrumbs,
  plus 1/2 cup for topping
- 1/8 cup of heavy cream
- 1 teaspoon of salt
- 1 teaspoon of black pepper
- 1/4 cup of grated Parmesan cheese
- 1 tablespoon of minced parsley

1. In a large stockpot, boil mirlitons until tender, about 45 minutes. Remove and cool.

2. Cut in half, remove pit area and discard pit.

3. Scoop out mirliton meat, leaving shells intact.

4. Cut mirliton meat in small cubes; set aside.

5. In a large sauté pan, melt butter over medium-high heat. Sauté onion, bellpepper and garlic.

6. Add ground beef and sauté until browned.

7. Add one cup of breadcrumbs and mirliton meat, then moisten with heavy cream.

8. Add salt, pepper and cheese. Stir thoroughly.

9. Place shells on baking sheet and fill with mirliton mixture. Sprinkle tops with breadcrumbs and parsley.

10. Bake uncovered for 20 to 30 minutes in a 350-degree oven until tops brown.

Serves four.

– Jacques Duffourc
French Quarter, New Orleans

Lasagna

Every New Orleans Italian family has its beloved recipe for this baked pasta party favorite, which sometimes takes its place right beside the turkey at Thanksgiving. Here's a recipe that makes us mighty thankful to the Italians.

- ½ pound of ground beef
- ½ pound of ground pork or veal
- 2 cloves of garlic, minced
- ¼ cup of minced onion
- 3 tablespoons of chopped parsley, divided
- 1 tablespoon of chopped basil
- 1½ teaspoons of Creole seasoning
- 2 cups of chopped tomatoes
- 2 small cans of tomato paste
- 1 (1-pound) package of lasagna noodles
- 2 (12 ounce) cartons of ricotta
  or cream-style cottage cheese
- 2 eggs, beaten
- 2 teaspoons of salt
- ½ teaspoon of black pepper
- ½ cup of grated Parmesan cheese
- 1 cup of grated mozzarella cheese

1. In a large saucepot, brown meats slowly, then drain off rendered fat.

2. Stir-in garlic, onion, one tablespoon of parsley, basil, Creole seasoning, tomatoes and tomato paste.

3. Simmer this meat sauce uncovered until thick, about 45 minutes.

4. Cook lasagna noodles according to directions on package, then rinse in cold water and drain.

5. In a bowl, combine ricotta or cottage cheese with eggs, salt, pepper, two tablespoons of parsley and Parmesan cheese.

6. Spread noodles to cover bottom of a large baking dish, followed by half the ricotta mixture, then half the mozzarella and half the meat sauce.

7. Repeat layers.

8. Bake lasagna in 375-degree oven for 30 minutes.

Seves eight to ten.

Meatballs & Spaghetti

Among the Sicilians of New Orleans, there's always a controversy about something. So you can bet there's a controversy about something as important as meatballs. There are all kinds of arguments about whether meatballs should be fried, baked or put in the red sauce raw. Every method can produce terrific meatballs. On the other hand, the main trick is to not roll them too much. Excess rolling will make meatballs tough.

- 4 pounds of ground beef
- 1½ cups of chopped onion
- 1½ cups of chopped bellpepper
- ½ cup of finely chopped parsley
- 1 tablespoon of coarse ground black pepper
- 1 tablespoon of salt
- 1 tablespoon of Italian seasoning
- 2 tablespoons of granulated garlic
- 2 eggs
- 1½ cups of Italian breadcrumbs
- Red Sauce (Recipe follows)
- 1 package of spaghetti, cooked according to directions on package

1. In a medium-size mixing bowl, blend ground beef with vegetables and spices. Add eggs and breadcrumbs.

2. For dinner-size meatballs, roll into 24 large meatballs.

3. Bake in 350-degree pre-heated oven for about 30 minutes.

4. Transfer meatballs into Red Sauce in a large saucepan and simmer for 20 minutes.

5. Serve over hot spaghetti.

RED SAUCE

- 4 tablespoons of olive oil
- 1½ cups of chopped green onion
- 1½ cups of chopped bellpepper
- ¼ of a garlic, peeled and chopped
- 1 gallon of tomato sauce
- ½ gallon of water
- 2 tablespoons of coarse ground black pepper
- 1 tablespoon of salt
- 1 teaspoon of crushed red pepper

1. Heat olive oil in a large saucepan, and sauté onion, bellpepper and garlic until translucent, about 10 minutes.

2. Add all other ingredients and bring to a boil.

3. Reduce heat, cover and simmer about one hour, stirring occasionally to prevent sticking.

Serves 10 to 12.

Panéed Veal

Back when veal was considered "poor folks' food," it didn't even get its name in the title. This was called just "panéed meat." Needless to say, veal gets its name in the title now.

- 4 (¼-inch thick) veal cutlets
- Salt, to taste
- Freshly ground black pepper, to taste
- 1 egg, beaten with 1 tablespoon of water
- ¾ cup of dry breadcrumbs
- 1 tablespoon of vegetable oil
- 1 tablespoon of butter
- Lemon wedges

1. Pound the cutlets with a mallet until they are thin and tender.

2. Season with salt and pepper, then dip into the egg mixture.

3. Coat with the breadcrumbs, then return to the egg mixture.

4. Heat the oil and butter in a skillet and sauté the cutlets on both sides until golden brown.

5. Drain on paper towels. Serve with lemon wedges.

Serves four.

Steak *au Poivre*

This is a French classic — and a New Orleans favorite when it comes time to switch from seafood to beef. The steak is wonderful, but this dish is all about the peppercorn-cognac sauce.

- 4 tablespoons of whole peppercorns
  (mixture of black, green, white, etc.)
- 4 filet mignons
- 3 tablespoons of butter, divided
- Salt, to taste
- 4 tablespoons of finely chopped green onions
- 1 cup of beef broth (low-sodium, if canned)
- 2/3 cup of cognac
- 5 or 6 tablespoons of softened butter

1. Crush the peppercorns on a cutting board using the bottom of a skillet, then press 'corns into the steaks.

2. Wrap steaks in waxed paper and refrigerate for about two hours.

3. Melt two tablespoons of butter in the skillet, season the steaks with salt, and cook until done to your liking.

4. Transfer the steaks to a hot platter and pour off any grease from the skillet.

5. Add an additional tablespoon of butter to the skillet and sauté green onions for about one minute.

6. Pour in the broth and cognac, stir, and scrape up browned bits from the bottom of the skillet.

7. Remove from heat and add softened butter, a tablespoon at a time, to enrich the sauce. Serve the steaks with the sauce poured over the top.

Serves four.

Fried Chicken I

It's a toss-up between Jacques Leonardi and Chef Austin Leslie of Jacques-Imo's or Heidi Trull of Elizabeth's for the greatest modern rendition of New Orleans fried chicken. But it would be safe to say that from Uptown to The Bywater, New Orleanians are widely known for preparing the world's best fried chicken.

- 12 ounces of whole milk
- 1 cup of water
- 1 egg, lightly beaten
- 1 teaspoon of salt
- 1 teaspoon of freshly ground black pepper
- 1 4-pound fryer, cut into serving pieces
- Salt and pepper, to season the chicken
- 1 cup of all-purpose flour
- 3 cups of oil for frying

1. Make a wash with the milk, water and egg.

2. Season the wash with a teaspoon of salt and a teaspoon of pepper.

3. Rinse the chicken under cold running water, then season it with salt and pepper.

4. To make the coating, dip the chicken pieces in the egg wash and then in the flour.

5. Place the chicken in 350-degree oil in a large cast iron skillet and fry, turning often until golden brown, about 25 minutes.

6. Remove from the skillet and drain on paper towels or brown paper bag.

Serves four.

Fried Chicken II

Yes, New Orleans is the first home to one of the world's most famous fried chicken chains. But back before Popeye became more than just another sailor, Austin Leslie had learned to be more than just another New Orleans cook.

- 3-pound fryer, cut into serving pieces
- Salt and black pepper, to taste
- 1 egg, lightly beaten
- 1 cup of half-and-half
- 1 cup of water
- ½ cup of all-purpose flour
- 1½ cups of peanut oil for frying
- Chopped dill pickles
- 1 tablespoon of finely chopped garlic
- 1 tablespoon of finely chopped fresh parsley

1. Wash the chicken pieces under cold running water and pat them dry. Season with salt and pepper.

2. In a bowl, combine egg, cream and water, sprinkling with salt and pepper.

3. Dip chicken pieces in egg wash, then in the flour. Shake off excess.

4. Place chicken in 350-degree oil in a deep fryer or frying pan, meatiest cuts going in first. Do not overcrowd the fryer. Turn pieces to brown on all sides.

5. Cook 10 to 12 minutes, or until meat is tender and batter is crisp.

6. Serve garnished with pickles, garlic and parsley.

Serves four.

– Chef Austin Leslie
Jacques-Imo's
New Orleans

Chicken Spaghetti

The Crescent City is full of "home remedies" — just the right medicine for an easy meal that's long on flavor. This written recipe may not impress you much, but the flavors that end up on the plate sure will.

- 8 ounces of cooked spaghetti
- 2 cups of boneless chicken breast, cooked and cut in small pieces
- 2 tablespoons of roasted red pepper
- 11 ounces of cream of mushroom soup
- ½ of a green bellpepper, diced small
- 1½ cups of American cheese, shredded
- ½ cup of mayonnaise

1. Preheat oven to 350 degrees.

2. Mix all ingredients together and pour into a large glass baking dish or casserole pan.

3. Cover and bake for about an hour.

Serves six to eight.

– Nolan V. Ferraro
Harahan (Jefferson Parish)

Chicken *Bonne Femme*

Literally translated as "Chicken Good Woman," this dish has both Creole and Cajun influences and capitalizes on the one-pot cooking technique used for red beans and rice and jambalaya. You can leave out the lemon if you desire or add more vegetables to the pot. You can even use a crock pot for this and slow-cook the recipe for eight to ten hours.

- 1 whole young hen, about four pounds
- ½ cup of apple-smoked bacon, diced
- 20 small pearl onions
- Zest of ½ lemon
- ½ cup of chicken stock
- Salt and black pepper, to taste
- ½ teaspoon of fresh thyme
- 1 pound of new potatoes, scrubbed clean and cut in half
- ½ pound of baby carrots
- 1 tablespoon of minced parsley
- 1 tablespoon of minced chives

1. Rinse chicken and bind the legs. Preheat oven to 400 degrees.

2. In a large roasting pan, fry bacon on the stove top. Brown chicken in roasting pan in the bacon fat over medium heat.

3. Add onions, lemon zest and chicken stock to the pan. Season the chicken with salt and pepper. Sprinkle chicken with thyme. Cover and bake for 30 minutes.

4. Add potatoes and carrots. Cover and bake for 25 minutes more or until chicken is tender.

5. Garnish with parsley and chives.

Serves four.

Chicken Stew

It's amazing how readily available ingredients and reasonably simple techniques can combine to make everyday foods taste anything but ordinary. Here's a version that might be called chicken stew — or, with the tomatoes, might be called chicken Creole.

- 1/4 cup of all-purpose flour
- 1 tablespoon of Creole seasoning
- 1/8 teaspoon of cayenne pepper
- 2 skinless, boneless chicken breast halves,
  cut into pieces
- 3 skinless, boneless chicken thighs,
  cut into pieces
- 2 tablespoons of butter, divided
- 1 tablespoon of vegetable oil
- 1 tablespoon of minced garlic
- 8 green onions, coarsely chopped
- 1 rib of celery, finely chopped
- 1 large green bellpepper, seeded and diced
- 1 14-ounce can of stewed tomatoes,
  undrained
- 1/2 cup of chicken broth
- 1 teaspoon of Tabasco sauce
- 1 bay leaf
- 1/4 pound of kielbasa sausage,
  sliced in ½-inch rounds

1. Combine flour, Creole seasoning and cayenne in a large bowl. Coat chicken lightly with flour mixture. Reserve excess flour for later.

2. In a large soup pot, heat one tablespoon of butter over medium-high heat. Add the chicken and cook until browned, about three minutes on each side. Remove chicken and place on a plate or dish of some kind. (Do not place on a paper towel. You will want to add the juices back to the stew at the end. Just set the chicken aside.)

3. Add one tablespoon of butter and one tablespoon of vegetable oil to the pot and heat over high heat. Add the garlic and sauté until you smell the garlic cooking, about one minute.

4. Add the remaining flour and stir until it dissolves into the butter and oils.

5. Add the green onions, celery and bellpepper. Cook until the vegetables begin to soften, five to seven minutes.

6. Add stewed tomatoes and juice, chicken broth, hot pepper sauce and bay leaf and bring to a boil. Reduce heat and simmer, stirring once or twice, until the vegetables are fully cooked, about 15 minutes.

7. Return the stew to a boil over medium-high heat. Return the chicken (and any juices that have accumulated on the plate) to the pot along with the sausage, and heat until the chicken is cooked through, about five minutes. Remove the bay leaf before serving.

8. Serve over cooked rice.

Serves six.

– Jen Plourde
French Quarter, New Orleans

Chicken Sauce Piquant

According to the Merriam-Webster dictionary, piquant is "agreeably stimulating to the palate; especially spicy or engagingly provocative." You'll find many Creole dishes fit this description, and many New Orleanians themselves seem to fit the latter definition. This piquant recipe seems to fill the bill as the most authentic and quintessential.

- 1 tablespoon of olive oil
- 3 or 4 chicken breasts, skinned and de-boned
- 2 large onions, finely chopped
- 1/4 cup of finely chopped celery
- 1/4 cup of finely chopped green bellpepper
- 2 cloves of fresh garlic, minced
- 3 tablespoons of all-purpose flour
- 8 ounces of tomato sauce
- 2 medium fresh tomatoes, seeded and chopped (1 cup)
- 8 ounces of canned green peas, drained
- 4 ounces of sliced mushrooms, drained
- 1/8 teaspoon of dried basil, crushed
- 1/2 teaspoon of cayenne pepper
- 1½ teaspoons of ground black pepper
- 1 bay leaf
- 1/4 cup of chopped green onions
- 3 tablespoons of finely chopped fresh parsley
- 2 cups of cooked white rice

1. Heat the oil over medium-high heat in a cast iron skillet. Brown the chicken on both sides. Set aside.

2. Add the onions, celery, green pepper and garlic and sauté until thoroughly cooked, 10 to 12 minutes.

3. Add the flour and continue to cook, stirring constantly until browned, eight to ten minutes.

4. Add the tomato sauce, fresh tomatoes, peas, mushrooms, basil, cayenne, black pepper and bay leaf. Reduce the heat and simmer for 10 minutes. Stir occasionally to keep sauce from sticking.

5. Return the chicken to the skillet, cover and continue to simmer for 25 minutes, or until the chicken is cooked through.

6. Stir-in the green onions and parsley and cook for an additional three minutes.

7. Remove from heat and serve over rice.

Serves four to six.

Chicken Fricassee

You can fricassee anything that doesn't fricassee you first! Fricassee is a real cooking term that means a dish in which the ingredients are first smothered or sautéed then simmered in a roux-based sauce.

- 1 4-pound chicken, cut into serving pieces
- ½ cup of all-purpose flour
- ½ cup of vegetable oil
- 5 green onions, chopped
- 1 onion, chopped
- 8 cups of chicken stock
- 5 stalks of celery, chopped
- 2 tablespoons of Creole seasoning
- ½ teaspoon of cayenne pepper
- 2 teaspoons of salt
- 2 teaspoons of ground black pepper
- 1 teaspoon of minced garlic
- 1 cup of brown roux

1. Wash chicken pieces under cold running water; pat dry with paper towels. Then roll chicken in flour to coat.

2. Heat one-half cup of oil in a large, deep skillet over medium-high heat. Fry chicken until thoroughly browned. Edges should be crispy.

3. Remove chicken and drain thoroughly.

4. Add all onions to skillet and sauté until cooked, about five minutes.

5. Return the chicken to the skillet. Add the stock and heat until bubbling.

6. Add the celery, Creole seasoning, cayenne pepper, salt, black pepper and minced garlic. Bring to a boil and reduce to a simmer, then continue to simmer for 25 minutes.

7. Add one-half cup of the roux and whisk to thoroughly incorporate. If sauce needs to be thicker, add the remaining roux. Reduce heat to low and continue to simmer uncovered for one and one-half hours.

8. Serve with rice.

Makes four to six servings.

*The architecture of downtown New Orleans
is quite similar to that of some European cities.*

Shrimp Creole

Generally, dishes called "Creole" are associated with tomatoes, and therefore associated with the city's under-recognized Spanish influence. Once you've tried true Shrimp Creole, you'll never be satisfied with a weak imitation.

- 1/4 pound of margarine
- 1 stalk of celery, diced
- 2 large bellpeppers, diced
- 2 large onions, diced
- 32 ounces (2 16-ounce cans) of crushed tomatoes
- 1 cup of beef stock
- 2 tablespoons of margarine
- 2 pounds of fresh shrimp, peeled and deveined
- 1/2 cup of chopped green onions
- 1 teaspoon of minced garlic
- 1/4 cup of shrimp stock
- 4 tablespoons of Creole seasoning

1. Heat margarine in a large stockpot over medium heat.

2. Sauté celery, bellpepper, and onion 10 to 12 minutes.

3. Add tomatoes and beef stock and simmer 30 minutes.

4. In a separate sauté pan over medium-high heat, melt two tablespoons of margarine. Sauté the shrimp with the green onions and garlic until the shrimp turn pink, about three to four minutes. Add the shrimp stock.

5. Add the cooked shrimp into the sauce, then add the Creole seasoning. Simmer for 20 to 25 minutes.

6. Remove from heat and serve over rice.

– Nolan V. Ferraro
Harahan (Jefferson Parish)

Boiled Shrimp

When shrimp are in season, it's common for New Orleanians to boil pounds upon pounds of them and spread them out on a table covered with newspaper.

- 2 gallons of water
- 4 tablespoons of yellow mustard seeds
- 3 tablespoons of coriander seeds
- 2 tablespoons of whole allspice
- 2 tablespoons of dill seeds
- 1 teaspoon of whole cloves
- 1 tablespoon of crushed red pepper
- 8 bay leaves
- 2 tablespoons of salt
- 1 teaspoon of cayenne pepper
- 2 pounds of fresh shrimp,
  whole and unpeeled, rinsed in cold water

1. Bring water to a boil in a large stockpot.

2. Combine all dry ingredients thoroughly, except salt and pepper. Place in a square of muslin or cheesecloth, tie securely with string, and add to boiling water.

3. Add salt and cayenne to the water.

4. Add shrimp and boil until cooked, until shells turn pink, approximately five minutes. Be careful not to overcook.

5. Remove from water, drain and cool.

6. Serve with your favorite dipping sauce.

Serves two.

– Jake Impastato Jr.
Lakeview (Orleans Parish)

Fried Shrimp

These fried shrimp are wonderful by themselves, sided by french fries and a zesty cocktail sauce. Or you can engage in "piling on" when you turn these into one of the city's favorite po-boys.

- 5 pounds of large shrimp, peeled and deveined
- 1 tablespoon of Creole seasoning
- 1½ cups of vegetable oil
- 6 eggs, beaten
- 1½ cups of all-purpose flour (You can substitute Zatarain's Fish Fry if you prefer.)

1. In a medium-size mixing bowl, season shrimp with Creole seasoning.

2. Heat oil in a medium-size cast iron skillet.

3. Dip shrimp in egg wash, then dredge in flour.

4. Fry until shrimp are golden brown, approximately five minutes.

5. Serve with your favorite dipping sauce or on po-boy bread, dressed.

– Jake Impastato Jr.
Lakeview (Orleans Parish)

Barbecued Shrimp I
(In the oven)

Only in New Orleans does barbecued shrimp mean no grill, no skewers and no barbecue sauce. Versions of this classic dish vary as much as the architecture and the people of the city. This recipe will put you on track, and you can adjust it to your own taste. If you want to try the original, venture to Pascal's Manale Restaurant on Napoleon Avenue.

- 5 pounds of large shrimp, heads on and unpeeled
- 1½ cups of spicy Italian dressing
- 1 cup of lemon juice
- 2 tablespoons of ground black pepper
- ¾ pound of butter

1. Rinse the shrimp. Make sure to leave heads on. This is the source of a lot of the flavor.

2. In a large glass baking dish, combine dressing, lemon juice and black pepper. Add shrimp, cover the dish, and marinate in the refrigerator overnight.

3. Add butter, re-cover and bake at 350 degrees for 30 minutes. Remove from the oven, uncover and cool for 15 minutes.

4. Serve with French bread for dipping – and lots of napkins.

Serves four to six.

Barbecued Shrimp II
(In the skillet)

The signature dish of Pascal's Manale Restaurant, this recipe combines the French love affair with butter, the Italian love affair with garlic and herbs, and maybe the Cajun love affair with heat into a single dish. Have lots of French bread on hand for sopping up the sauce.

- ½ cup of butter
- 4 pounds of shrimp, heads on and unpeeled
- ½ cup of zesty Italian dressing
- 1 tablespoon of lemon juice
- 2 teaspoons of ground black pepper
- 10 cloves of garlic, peeled
- 1 teaspoon of cayenne pepper
- 1 teaspoon of crushed red pepper
- 1 tablespoon of Worcestershire sauce

1. In a large skillet over medium-high heat, melt the butter.

2. Add the shrimp and sauté until shrimp turn pink, about five minutes.

3. Add the remaining ingredients and stir well to fully incorporate.

4. Reduce heat to low and simmer for 20 minutes, or until garlic is soft.

5. Remove from heat and serve with French bread for dipping.

Serves three or four.

Stuffed Shrimp

Preparing a stuffing is one of the basic kitchen skills New Orleans mothers teach their daughters. The same stuffing can be used in stuffed crabs, stuffed flounder, and these wonderful stuffed shrimp.

- 36 fresh jumbo shrimp, about 3 pounds
- Salt and black pepper, to taste
- Crabmeat Stuffing (Recipe follows)
- 2 cups of all-purpose flour
- Egg wash (3 eggs mixed with 1½ cups of milk)
- Seasoned breadcrumbs
- Vegetable oil for frying
- Chopped fresh parsley

1. Peel the shrimp, but leave the fantails on.

2. Season shrimp with salt and pepper.

3. Take about one tablespoon of Crabmeat Stuffing for each shrimp, flattening it in the palm of your hand and forming it tightly around the shrimp.

4. Coat shrimp in flour and dip it into egg wash and then into the breadcrumbs.

5. Brown evenly in a frying pan in vegetable oil for about 10 minutes, turning regularly so all sides are golden.

6. Garnish with parsley.

Serves 12.

CRABMEAT STUFFING

- 1 stick of butter
- 5 sprigs of fresh parsley, chopped
- 1 rib of celery, finely chopped
- 1 small green bellpepper, finely chopped
- 1 large onion, finely chopped
- 2 teaspoons of finely chopped garlic
- 1 teaspoon of dried thyme
- Salt and black pepper, to taste
- 1 pound of picked crabmeat
- 1 loaf of day-old French bread, soaked in water, then water pressed out by hand
- 3 eggs, lightly beaten

1. In a skillet, melt the butter and sauté the parsley, celery, bellpepper, onion, garlic and thyme, seasoning with salt and pepper.

2. Add the crabmeat and sauté an additional 10 minutes. Let mixture cool.

3. In a bowl, mash the soaked bread with your hands until mushy, seasoning with salt and pepper.

4. Add the cooked crabmeat and vegetables along with the eggs; mix gently.

5. Transfer this mixture to a baking pan, cover with foil and bake at 350 degrees for one hour, stirring after about 30 minutes.

6. Remove from the oven and refrigerate until cold.

Fried Oysters

It's the thing in New Orleans. From the Acme Oyster House in the French Quarter and Casamento's Uptown to Deanie's at the Lakefront, oysters are king in New Orleans.

- 2 dozen shucked oysters
- 2 eggs
- 2/3 cup of whole milk
- 1 tablespoon of Creole seasoning
- 1/2 teaspoon of garlic powder
- 1/2 teaspoon of onion powder
- 1 teaspoon of Tabasco
- 1 teaspoon of cayenne pepper
- Salt and fresh ground black pepper, to taste
- 2 cups of cornmeal
- 1/4 cup of cornstarch
- 2 tablespoons of Creole seasoning
- 1/2 teaspoon of salt
- 1/2 teaspoon of black pepper
- 1/2 teaspoon of cayenne pepper
- 1 teaspoon of lemon-pepper seasoning
- Peanut oil for frying

1. Gently rinse the oysters and keep them on ice or in the refrigerator.

2. Make a marinade by combining the next eight ingredients.

3. Place marinade in a large non-reactive bowl. Transfer oysters to mixture and refrigerate for at least one hour.

4. Make a breading mixture by combining the next seven ingredients. Place these ingredients in a gallon zip-lock bag and shake vigorously to mix.

5. In a large frying pan, heat peanut oil to 350-375 degrees. Make sure you have at least two inches depth of oil in the pan.

6. Place a few oysters at a time in the breading mixture and leave them there for a minute to make sure the breading sticks.

7. Add a few oysters at a time to the hot oil. Leave plenty of space between them. Don't add the oysters all at once or the oil will cool too much and you'll have soggy oysters.

8. Cook the oysters for about four or five minutes. Let them cook until the oil barely bubbles. Do not judge by the color of the breading; it is all about the bubbles.

9. Remove oysters from skillet and place on paper towels to drain.

Serves four.

Oysters Bienville

If Antoine's always rightly laid claim to creating Oysters Rockefeller, Arnaud's on Bienville Street presented the most convincing case for creating Oysters Bienville. This baked oyster classic goes back as far as the 1920s or 1930s, when the restaurant was still operated by its oh-so-charismatic founder, known locally as Count Arnaud.

- 1 box of rock salt
- 6 aluminum pie pans
- 3 dozen cleaned oyster shells
- 3 dozen oysters, shucked
- Bienville Sauce (Recipe follows)
- 1/2 cup of unseasoned breadcrumbs
- 1/2 cup of grated Parmesan cheese, to garnish
- 2 tablespoons of butter, melted

1. Pour rock salt in each pie pan to make a half-inch bed.

2. Place six oyster shells in each pie pan.

3. Place one oyster in each shell. Spoon one to two ounces of Bienville Sauce in each shell. Top with breadcrumbs and Parmesan cheese and drizzle with melted butter.

4. Fill all of the shells in the same manner.

5. Bake in a 350-degree oven for five to seven minutes or until edges of oysters curl.

6. Remove from oven and serve.

BIENVILLE SAUCE

- 3 slices of uncooked bacon, chopped
- 2 tablespoons of butter
- 1/4 cup of all-purpose flour
- 2 cups of milk
- 8 ounces of American cheese, grated
- 1/3 cup of chopped green onions
- 1/4 cup of dry sherry
- 1/4 teaspoon of Worcestershire sauce
- 1/4 teaspoon of white pepper
- Dash of Tabasco sauce

1. In a large skillet, sauté bacon until edges curl and meat is light brown.

2. Add butter and flour and cook over low heat, stirring constantly until a white roux is formed; do not brown.

3. Add milk gradually to make a smooth sauce.

4. Cook over low heat until sauce thickens and bubbles.

5. Stir-in cheese and cook until melted.

6. Add remaining ingredients and stir to combine. Remove from heat.

Serves six.

– Jacques Duffourc
French Quarter, New Orleans

Oysters Rockefeller

Of all the baked oyster dishes created in New Orleans, this one, associated with Antoine's in the French Quarter, enjoys a certain pride of place. Antoine's recipe is still a secret, though the family explains the dish got its name for being as "rich as Rockefeller."

- ¼ pound of bacon, chopped
- ½ medium onion, diced
- ½ tablespoon of minced garlic
- ¼ tablespoon of salt
- ¼ tablespoon of freshly cracked black pepper
- ¼ tablespoon of tarragon
- ¼ tablespoon of thyme
- 1 dash of cayenne pepper
- ½ ounce of Pernod
- 1¼ pounds of spinach, blanched and squeezed dry
- 1 egg white
- ¼ tablespoon of heavy cream
- 2 tablespoons of Creole mustard
- ½ cup of grated Parmesan cheese
- 24 oysters, shucked and detached from the shell, but leaving oyster on the half shell

1. Preheat the broiler oven.

2. Heat a large skillet over high heat and brown the bacon.

3. Add the onion and cook for three to four minutes. Add the garlic, spices and herbs. Reduce heat and sauté for another five to seven minutes.

4. Deglaze the pan with Pernod.

5. Add spinach and mix well.

6. Remove mixture from heat and chill for 15 to 20 minutes.

7. Add remaining ingredients (except oysters) and mix well.

8. Arrange the oysters on their half shells on a baking pan. Top each oyster with a spoonful of the stuffing mix.

9. Broil for five to seven minutes, or until stuffing is bubbling.

Serves four.

Oyster Loaf
('The Peacemaker')

Why eat a mere oyster po-boy when you can munch on a "peacemaker." That would be mediatrice *in French — the one dish New Orleans husbands have always brought home to make up with their wives after a spat.*

- 2 tablespoons of butter
- 1 large loaf of French bread, sliced in half lengthwise and hollowed out
- 10 dill pickle slices
- Fried Oysters (See recipe on page 118)

1. Cut French bread in half horizontally and make indentations in both halves by scooping out about half of the bread.

2. Melt butter and spread generously on both sides of the bread.

3. Place pickles on bottom layer.

4. Fill the bottom of the hollowed-out loaf with a heaping layer of hot fried oysters.

5. Spread ketchup or cocktail sauce on top layer.

6. Put the loaf together and heat it in a 300-degree oven for a few minutes. Cut loaf into two- or three-inch slices. Serve hot.

Serves two to four.

Crabmeat *Au Gratin*

The tradition of crabmeat baked beneath cheese has truly found a home in New Orleans. Here's a perfect rendition of a dish with which New Orleanians seem to be fascinated.

- 2 sticks of butter
- 1/2 cup of chopped celery
- 1 large onion, chopped
- 1/2 cup of all-purpose flour
- 13 ounces of evaporated milk
- 1 teaspoon of salt
- 1/8 teaspoon of cayenne pepper
- 2 egg yolks
- 1 pound of jumbo lump crabmeat, picked over for shells and cartilage
- 1/2 cup of cheddar cheese

1. Preheat oven to 325 degrees.

2. In a large sauté pan, heat butter on high heat. Sauté celery and onion until translucent, five to seven minutes.

3. Add flour and stir.

4. Add milk slowly and cook on medium-high heat until thickened, about five minutes. Stir constantly.

5. Add salt, pepper and yolks. Stir.

6. Add crabmeat and gently stir to combine.

7. Pour into an oven-proof casserole dish, top with cheese and bake uncovered until cheese bubbles and begins to brown, 25 to 30 minutes.

Makes four servings.

– John "Bom" & Mignon Perrotta
French Quarter, New Orleans

Stuffed Crabs

A crab boil in New Orleans can be a many-splendored thing — and a many-meal thing as well. Be sure you boil enough crabs to eat your fill, and to have enough left over to peel and pick for the host of wonders to come.

- 1 onion, finely chopped
- 4 green onions, finely chopped
- 1 stick of butter, plus additional butter
- 1/2 cup of seasoned breadcrumbs, plus additional seasoned breadcrumbs
- 1 tablespoon of minced parsley
- 1/2 cup of half-and-half
- 1 tablespoon of dry sherry
- 2 cups of lump crabmeat, picked over for shells and cartilage
- Salt and black pepper, to taste
- 1/8 teaspoon of ground red pepper
- 1/8 teaspoon of ground thyme
- 8 cleaned crab shells
- Juice of 1 lemon

1. Sauté the onion and green onion in one stick of butter, then add one-half cup of breadcrumbs and mix thoroughly.

2. Add parsley, half-and-half, sherry and crabmeat, combining gently to preserve the lumps of crabmeat.

3. Season with salt, peppers and thyme. Let mixture cool.

4. Coat the inside of each crab shell with a little additional butter, then fill with the stuffing.

5. Sprinkle lightly with additional breadcrumbs and dot with additional butter.

6. Spoon a little lemon juice on top and bake uncovered at 325 degrees until tops turn golden brown, about 15 minutes.

Serves eight.

Boiled Crabs

Okay, so there's shrimp season and crawfish season, when these delicious seafoods take their turns in the great big melting pot called New Orleans. And when crabs are in season, they are as popular as their relatives at other times of the year.

SEASONING FOR WATER

- 1 8-ounce bottle of liquid crab boil
- 1 (3-pound) box of Morton's Kosher salt
- 6 lemons, cut in half
- 6 satsuma oranges, cut in quarters (optional)
- 1 large onion, cut in quarters
- 1 large garlic bulb, cut in half
- 20 bay leaves
- 1 tablespoon of cayenne (optional)

Prepare ingredients and add to the water once it begins to boil.

Note: This will season eight to ten gallons of water. Adjust accordingly.

VEGETABLES

- 4 large onions, quartered
- 3 pounds of small red potatoes, rinsed and left whole
- 4 bunches of garlic, pods cut in half to expose the meat
- 10 shucked ears of corn, cut in thirds
- 5 cups of fresh button mushrooms

1. Divide the vegetables in half and place into two separate mesh bags appropriate for cooking in high temperature. An onion sack works pretty well for this.

2. Cook the first batch of vegetables by placing the entire sack in the boiling water. (Note: The first batch of vegetables will be pretty spicy. Save the second batch for later for a less spicy version.)

126

To clean live crabs:

- 4 or 5 dozen live crabs

1. In a large tub with some type of drainage, rinse the crabs thoroughly with water. Watch out for the pinchers!

2. If the crabs come from a sandy area, be sure to soak them for 30 to 45 minutes in clean water to remove the sand. (Never use soap or cleaning fluid on the crabs!)

To boil:

1. In a large kettle with a basket liner appropriate for boiling seafood, bring the seasoned water to a boil. Add the first sack of vegetables.

2. Add the first batch of live crabs and boil for ten minutes. Crab shells will turn bright orange.

3. Turn off fire.

4. At this point you want to let the water cool down so the crabs will stop cooking and soak in the seasoning. Same for the vegetables. You can do this by adding two gallon jugs of cold water you've cooled in the freezer.

5. Also, you want to stir the crabs around, then let them sit and soak for at least 15 minutes.

6. Taste and check for seasoning. If they need more seasoning, let them continue to soak, checking every five minutes or so, until they taste the way you want them to. The longer they soak the more the seasoning will set.

(Continued on next page)

7. Remove the crabs and sack of vegetables from the seasoned water using the basket liner. Dump in an empty, clean ice chest and leave the lid cracked so the crabs and vegetables can cool. Or dump directly on a newspaper-lined table along with the vegetables — and dig in!

8. Reserve the water and repeat the process until all the crabs and the second sack of vegetables are cooked.

Note: Figure five to eight crabs per person — or more depending on the size. Always purchase live crabs from a reputable place. Crabs are graded according to size. Ask a few questions so you end up with sweet, meaty crabs.

— Donald Duke Jr.
Chalmette (St. Bernard Parish)

Fried Soft-Shell Crabs

You can get soft-shell crabs around New Orleans almost anytime of year now, thanks to creative capitalists out in the marsh who love to fool with Mother Nature. The much more recently developed soft-shell crawfish are great cooked this way, too.

- 6 soft-shell crabs
- 1 cup of milk
- 1 egg
- Creole seasoning, to taste
- 1 cup of all-purpose flour
- Vegetable oil for deep-frying
- Lemon slices
- Chopped parsley

1. Clean and prepare the crabs according to the following method: With a pair of kitchen shears, cut each crab accross the face. Remove the eye sockets and the lower mouth. Carefully lift up the top shell and remove the gills. Rinse crabs with cool water and pat them dry.

2. Combine the milk and egg, adding seasoning.

3. Soak crabs in this mixture for one hour.

4. Coat lightly in flour, shake off excess and deep-fry in 350-degree oil until golden brown, three to five minutes, until crabs float to the surface and are golden brown.

5. Garnish with lemon slices and chopped parsley.

Serves six.

Crab Sardou

French playwright Victorien Sardou visited New Orleans at the height of his fame – and inspired one of the city's most famous brunch dishes, Eggs Sardou. This lush crab dish takes all the main elements of that classic, but shows up delicious without the eggs.

- 12 artichokes
- Hollandaise Sauce (Recipe follows)
- Creamed Spinach (Recipe follows)
- 2 pounds of jumbo lump crabmeat, picked over for shells and cartilage
- 1 cup of clarified butter

1. In a large pot, submerge the artichokes in water and boil for approximately 30 minutes, until the stems are tender.

2. Allow the artichokes to cool, and peel the leaves from the hearts. Using a spoon or your thumb, remove and discard the hearts, leaving the bottoms of the artichokes.

3. While waiting for the artichokes to cook and cool, prepare the Hollandaise Sauce and Creamed Spinach.

4. Sauté the crabmeat in the clarified butter until hot, being careful not to break the lumps. Remove from heat.

5. Arrange serving plates and spoon equal portions of the Creamed Spinach onto the plates. Place two peeled artichoke bottoms into the bed of spinach.

6. Drain excess butter from the crabmeat, and spoon equal portions into the cavities of the artichoke bottoms.

7. Finally, top with a generous portion of the Hollandaise Sauce.

Serves six.

HOLLANDAISE SAUCE

- 6 egg yolks
- 7 tablespoons of solid butter, cut into small pieces
- Pinch of salt
- Pinch of cayenne pepper
- 1 teaspoon of lemon juice
- 1 teaspoon of red wine vinegar
- 2 cups of clarified butter
- 2 tablespoons of cold water

1. In a double boiler over medium heat, combine egg yolks with butter, salt, cayenne pepper, lemon juice and red wine vinegar.

2. Whisk the ingredients continuously until the mixture increases in volume and achieves a consistency that adheres to the whisk.

3. Using a ladle, slowly add the clarified butter while continuing to slowly whisk the butter into the mixture. (If the sauce appears to be too thick, add a touch of the cold water to bring it back to a proper consistency.)

CREAMED SPINACH

- 3 cups of cooked spinach
- 1 cup of Béchamel Sauce (Recipe follows)
- Salt and pepper, to taste

In a sauté pan, combine the spinach and Béchamel Sauce and simmer over low heat. Season to taste.

BÉCHAMEL SAUCE

- 1 cup of milk
- 4 tablespoons of butter
- ½ cup of all-purpose flour

1. Heat milk until it simmers.

2. In a separate pan, melt the butter over medium-high heat and add the flour to make a roux.

(Continued on next page)

3. Continue whisking on a low heat to cook the flour but do not allow it to remain on the heat long enough to change from a blonde roux to a brown roux.

4. Add one-half of the heated milk to the roux while constantly whisking. This mixture will become thick like a paste. Add the remaining milk and whisk until smooth.

– Galatoire's Restaurant
French Quarter, New Orleans

Crawfish *Etouffee*

Here's one of the classic New Orleans dishes that trekked in from Cajun country. The word etouffee *means "smothered," referring to the simmering that turns the crawfish stew into something that is truly delicious.*

- 1 stick of butter
- 1 large onion, chopped
- 1/2 bellpepper, chopped
- 2 ribs of celery, chopped
- 1 teaspoon of minced garlic
- 2 pounds of crawfish tails, peeled and deveined
- 1 teaspoon of lemon juice
- 1 teaspoon of salt
- 1/2 teaspoon of black pepper
  (or 1 teaspoon of Creole seasoning)
- 1/8 cup of water

1. In a large sauté pan, melt butter over medium-high heat.

2. Add onion, bellpepper, celery and garlic. Sauté until cooked, about 10 minutes.

3. Add crawfish, lemon juice, salt, pepper and water. Bring to a boil, reduce to a simmer.

4. Continue to simmer until *etouffee* thickens, 10 to 15 minutes. Serve over white rice.

Boiled Crawfish

Boiled Crawfish is one of those foods that is synonymous with New Orleans and all of south Louisiana. With the traditional backyard crawfish boil, friends and family members while away the hours enjoying the food and the company; it is an art form of relaxation that has gone on for generations.

- 30 quarts of cold water
- 12 medium onions, quartered
- 6 heads of garlic, split in half, exposing pods
- 6 lemons, quartered
- 1 cup of cooking oil
- 4 pounds of salt
- ½ pound of cayenne pepper
- 4 (3-ounce) bags of Zatarain's crab boil
- 6 tablespoons of celery salt
- 24 medium red potatoes
- 12 ears of corn
- 50 pounds of cleaned crawfish

1. In a 60-quart stock pot, bring water to a rolling boil.

2. Add onions, garlic, lemons, cooking oil, salt, pepper, Zatarain's crab boil and celery salt and continue to boil for 30 minutes. This boiling of the vegetables will ensure a good flavor in the boiling liquid.

3. Add red potatoes and cook approximately 10 to 12 minutes.

4. Add corn and cook 10 minutes.

5. Remove corn and potatoes from the pot and put them in an ice chest or bucket to keep them warm.

6. Once the water returns to a boil, cook crawfish seven to ten minutes, turn off heat and allow crawfish to set in hot liquid 12 additional minutes. Serve crawfish hot with potatoes and corn.

– Chef John Folse

Blackened Redfish

World-renowned Cajun Chef Paul Prudhomme created this dish in the 1980s and turned it into something of a national phenomenon. It has such a sensational taste that visitors to the city would stand in line for an hour or more to get a seat in his New Orleans restaurant, K-Paul's Louisiana Kitchen. This recipe was supplied not by Chef Paul but by another New Orleans resident with considerable culinary talent.

- 1 tablespoon of all-purpose flour
- 1 teaspoon of paprika
- 1/4 teaspoon of cayenne
- 1/2 teaspoon of salt
- 1 teaspoon of black pepper
- Dash of thyme
- 1 teaspoon of garlic powder
- 4 (6-ounce) fillets of redfish, black drum or catfish
- 1 tablespoon of vegetable oil
- 1 whole lemon, thinly sliced to garnish

1. Combine dry ingredients in a mixing bowl.

2. Heat a cast iron skillet over high heat.

3. Brush fillets lightly with vegetable oil and coat with seasoning.

4. Fry fillets in the cast iron skillet for approximately two minutes on each side, until coating begins to blacken. Turn only once and cook on the other side.

5. Remove from pan and serve with a lemon garnish.

Note: Do not add oil to the skillet; this technique requires a dry skillet.

– Noel Rideout
Faubourg Marigny District
New Orleans

Trout Amandine

The marriage of lush butter and crisp almonds makes for an unforgettable topping on this simple sautéed fresh speckled trout.

- 6 speckled trout fillets, 8 ounces each
- 1 cup of cold milk
- 1 cup of all-purpose flour, seasoned with salt and cayenne pepper
- 1 stick of butter
- Amandine Sauce (Recipe follows)

1. Soak the trout fillets in milk for about 10 minutes.

2. Dredge the soaked trout in seasoned flour, shaking off excess.

3. Melt the butter in a heavy frying pan and fry the fish on each side just until golden, about four minutes per side.

4. Serve the fish and top with Amandine Sauce.

AMANDINE SAUCE

- ¾ stick of butter
- 1½ cups of thinly sliced almonds
- ¼ cup of fresh lemon juice
- 2 tablespoons of chopped fresh parsley
- Salt and black pepper, to taste

1. Melt the butter in a pan, add the almonds and stir until almonds are golden brown, three to four minutes.

2. Add the lemon juice and parsley, seasoning to taste with salt and pepper. Simmer two to three minutes to thicken. Keep warm.

Serves six.

– Arnaud's Restaurant
French Quarter, New Orleans

Trout Meuniere

In New Orleans seafood restaurants, ranging from very plain to very fancy, this is one of the favorite ways to enjoy the area's wonderful speckled trout. The fish gets delicately batter-fried, then turned to glory with a simple sauce based on butter and lemon.

- 2 eggs
- 1 cup of all-purpose flour
- 1 tablespoon of Creole seasoning
- 4 6-ounce trout fillets
- 1 stick of butter
- Meuniere Sauce (Recipe follows)
- Fresh parsley

1. Whisk the eggs in a small bowl. Set aside.

2. In a separate bowl, mix flour with Creole seasoning.

3. Dredge trout fillets in egg wash then flour mixture. Shake off excess.

4. Heat butter in a large skillet. Fry trout fillets three minutes on each side. Remove and drain on paper towels.

5. To serve, top warm trout fillets with the Meuniere Sauce. Garnish with fresh parsley.

MEUNIERE SAUCE

- ¾ cup of butter
- 3 tablespoons of freshly squeezed lemon juice
- ¼ teaspoon of salt
- 1 dash of Tabasco
- 2 tablespoons of chopped green onion
- 1 tablespoon of minced parsley
- ¼ teaspoon of white pepper
- Dash of Worcestershire sauce

1. Melt butter in a saucepan over medium heat. Add lemon juice, salt and hot sauce and cook for one minute.

2. Add green onion, parsley, pepper and Worcestershire. Stir and simmer for five minutes.

Serves four.

– John Dunn and Katie Wells
Faubourg Marigny District
New Orleans

Stuffed Flounder

Yes, this is the absolute best way to eat the delicate, flat fish that's caught near New Orleans, usually at night right close to the shore.

- 6 flounder
- Egg wash (3 eggs mixed with 1½ cups of milk)
- Corn flour
- Stuffing (Recipe follows)
- 4 tablespoons of breadcrumbs
- 3 tablespoons of paprika
- 3 tablespoons of butter

1. After flounder are cleaned, use a sharp knife to separate the top fillet from the bones, forming a pocket for the Stuffing.

2. Dip each flounder in egg wash, then in corn flour, shaking off excess flour.

3. Deep-fry for about five minutes, then transfer to a baking dish or ovenproof platter.

4. Stuff each flounder with the Stuffing.

5. In a bowl, combine the breadcrumbs with the paprika and sprinkle this over the tops of the fish.

6. Dot with butter and bake at 350 degrees until Stuffing is heated through, about eight minutes.

STUFFING

- 1 stick of butter
- 5 sprigs of fresh parsley, chopped
- 1 rib of celery, finely chopped
- 1 small green bellpepper, finely chopped
- 1 large onion, finely chopped
- 2 teaspoons of finely chopped garlic
- 1 teaspoon of dried thyme
- Salt and black pepper, to taste
- 1 dozen fresh oysters
- 1 loaf of day-old French bread,
  soaked in liquor from oysters
- 3 eggs, lightly beaten

1. In a skillet, melt the butter and sauté the parsley, celery, bellpepper, onion, garlic and thyme, seasoning with salt and pepper.

2. Add the oysters and sauté an additional 10 minutes. Let mixture cool.

3. In a bowl, mash the soaked bread with your hands until soft, seasoning with salt and pepper.

4. Add the cooked oysters and vegetables along with the eggs; mix well.

5. Transfer this mixture to a baking pan, cover with foil, and bake at 350 degrees for one hour, stirring after about 30 minutes. Remove from the oven and let cool.

Serves six.

Pompano en Papillote

Created at Antoine's and named in honor of a French balloonist, this dish does indeed puff up like a balloon in the oven. Though the dish may be prepared in a somewhat unusual way, the result is an exceptionally tasty meal.

- 4 medium pompano fillets
- 2 tablespoons of chopped onion
- 4 tablespoons of butter
- 1¾ cups of white wine
- 3/4 cup of picked crabmeat
- 3/4 cup of diced shrimp
- 1/2 clove of garlic, minced
- 1/8 teaspoons of crumbled thyme
- 1 bay leaf
- 1½ cups of fish stock
- 2 tablespoons of all-purpose flour
- Salt and white pepper
- Parchment paper
- Vegetable Oil

1. In a large skillet, sauté the pompano over medium heat with half the onion, half the butter and half the white wine.

2. Reduce heat, cover and simmer until tender, four to five minutes.

3. In a separate pan, gently sauté the crabmeat and shrimp with

the remaining half of onion, butter and white wine – plus garlic, thyme, bay leaf and fish stock.

4. Drain the liquid from the pompano and blend this liquid together with the flour.

5. Add this liquid to the crabmeat-shrimp mixture and simmer about 10 minutes, until thickened.

6. Season to taste with salt and pepper. Remove bay leaf.

7. Preheat oven to 450 degrees.

8. Cut parchment into four heart shapes, about 12 inches long and eight inches wide. Brush the paper with vegetable oil.

9. Spoon a quarter of the crabmeat-shrimp mixture into the center of each heart and top with a fillet of pompano. Fold the paper over to cover the fish and seal by folding the edges together.

10. Lay sealed papers on an oiled baking sheet and bake in oven for 12 to 14 minutes, until paper turns brown.

11. Serve immediately, cutting open parchment in front of each guest.

Serves four.

– Antoine's Restaurant
French Quarter, New Orleans

Redfish *Courtbouillon*

Here's a kicked-up spin on a dish that's as New Orleans as they come — a "short broth" in which our redfish gets simmered to juicy perfection.

- 1/2 cup of vegetable oil
- 5 tablespoons of all-purpose flour
- 2 large onions, chopped
- 3 cloves of garlic, minced
- 3 stalks of celery, chopped
- 1/4 cup of chopped bellpepper
- 1/2 cup of chopped green onion
- 1/4 cup of chopped fresh parsley
- 6 ounces of tomato paste
- 6 ounces of tomato sauce
- 1/4 cup of olive oil
- 1 tablespoon of Italian seasoning
- 1 tablespoon of sugar
- 1 cup of seafood stock
- 10 ounces of spicy diced tomatoes
  (Ro-Tel brand suggested)
- 2 pounds of fresh redfish fillets,
  cut in pieces

1. In a large saucepot, heat oil on medium-high heat. Add flour and stir until the consistency of the flour and oil mixture is like wet sand. Lower heat and stir constantly, cooking until you have a medium-brown roux.

2. Add onion, garlic and celery and sauté until cooked, approximately five minutes.

3. Add bellpepper, green onion and parsley. Continue to sauté until vegetables soften, about five minutes.

4. Add tomato paste, tomato sauce, olive oil, Italian seasoning and sugar. Continue to brown and stir constantly. Cook until oil forms a skin on the top, about 10 minutes.

5. Add seafood stock and spicy tomatoes and simmer on low heat for about two hours. (The longer you simmer this recipe the better the sauce will get.) Add more stock or water as needed.

6. Add redfish and continue to simmer for another 15 minutes or until the fish is cooked. Do not stir; stirring breaks up the fish.

7. Serve over rice.

Serves eight.

– Donald Duke Jr.
Chalmette (St. Bernard Parish)

Fried Fish

In the good old days, New Orleanians fried almost any fish but catfish. But with the availability of terrific mild-tasting, farm-raised catfish in every supermarket, this has become the heir apparent to any and all fried fish.

- 2 pounds of catfish, speckled trout or other mild, white-fleshed Gulf fish fillets
- 1 cup of yellow cornmeal
- 3/4 teaspoon of freshly ground black pepper
- 1/8 teaspoon of paprika
- 1/2 teaspoon of Creole seasoning
- Vegetable oil for frying

1. Rinse the fish fillets and pat them dry.

2. Combine the cornmeal with the seasonings in a medium bowl.

3. Preheat the oil in a skillet to 360 degrees.

4. Dredge the fish in the seasoned cornmeal, shaking off excess, and fry in the oil, two fillets at a time, for two to three minutes, just until golden brown.

5. Drain on paper towels, letting oil return to proper temperature before frying the next batch.

6. Serve with cocktail sauce.

Serves four.

Riverwalk, located at the foot of Canal Street, is a popular shopping destination.

Oyster Dressing

Deanie's Seafood Restaurant in Bucktown on the lakefront is known for its perfect fried seafood. This recipe is an adaptation of their oyster dressing.

- 4 ounces of butter
- 2 cups of finely chopped onion
- 1 cup of finely chopped celery
- 1 cup of thinly sliced green onion
- 1½ tablespoons of minced garlic
- 4 dozen oysters, drained and chopped
- ½ cup of finely chopped parsley
- 1 teaspoon of freshly ground black pepper
- ½ cup of grated Pecorino Romano cheese
- 3 cups of coarse unseasoned breadcrumbs, plus ½ cup for topping
- 1½ cups of oyster liquid

1. Melt the butter in a large saucepan over medium heat. Sauté the onion, celery, green onion and garlic until tender, about 10 minutes.

2. Gradually add the chopped oysters. Cook for five minutes, stirring constantly. Add the parsley, stir and lower the heat. Simmer for about five minutes.

3. Add the black pepper and cheese and stir to fully incorporate. Remove from heat.

4. Slowly add three cups of the breadcrumbs, then add the oyster liquid. Cover and let stand for about five minutes to allow the breadcrumbs to absorb the oyster liquid. Season with salt.

5. Transfer dressing to a buttered casserole dish. Finish the top with one-half cup of breadcrumbs and dots of butter.

6. Bake uncovered for 20 minutes in a 350-degree oven.

Serves six to eight.

Eggplant Dressing
with Shrimp & Crabmeat

Eggplant made it to New Orleans with the Sicilians, having made it to Sicily with the Greeks. It's safe to say we New Orleanians love eggplant — especially what happens in casseroles such as this.

- 2 pounds of medium shrimp, heads off
- 4 cups of water
- ½ pound of margarine
- 3 large onions, chopped fine
- 2 medium bellpeppers, chopped fine
- 2 stalks of celery, chopped fine
- 4 medium eggplants, peeled and cut into one-inch cubes
- 1½ teaspoons of cayenne pepper
- 1½ teaspoons of white pepper
- ½ teaspoon of black pepper
- 1½ teaspoons of salt
- 4 to 6 dashes of Tabasco sauce
- 1 teaspoon of dried thyme, or 1 tablespoon of fresh
- 1 pound of cooked crabmeat, claw or white
- 1 cup of chopped green onion
- 1 cup of chopped parsley
- ½ cup of grated Parmesan cheese
- ½ cup of breadcrumbs

1. Peel and devein the shrimp; set aside.

2. Place the peels in a small saucepan and add the water.

3. Bring to a boil and reduce by half over medium-high heat, boiling for 15 to 20 minutes. Strain and set aside.

148

4. Melt the margarine over medium-high heat in a Dutch oven or other large, heavy pot and add the onions, peppers, and celery. Cook the vegetables until they are very soft, stirring occasionally, 20 to 25 minutes.

5. Meanwhile, peel the eggplants and cut them into one-inch cubes.

6. Place eggplant in a saucepan and add just enough water to cover. Bring to a boil and boil slowly for a few minutes, just until tender. Drain.

7. Puree eggplant until smooth in a blender or food processor.

8. Add the eggplant, shrimp stock, seasonings, and herbs to the vegetable mixture, return to a simmer, and cook over medium heat for 10 minutes, stirring occasionally.

9. Add the shrimp and continue to cook over medium-high heat just until the shrimp turn pink, five to seven minutes.

10. Add the crabmeat and cook just long enough to heat through.

11. Remove from heat and stir-in green onion and parsley.

12. Spoon the hot dressing into a casserole or individual ramekins. Sprinkle the top generously with Parmesan cheese and breadcrumbs and glaze under the broiler for a couple of minutes, until the cheese melts and the tops begin to brown.

Serves six to eight.

– Chef Alex Patout
Alex Patout's Louisiana Restaurant
French Quarter, New Orleans

Mirliton Dressing

Sometimes you'll find these delicious vegetables sold in the market by their Hispanic name, chayote. But in New Orleans they're known as mirlitons — pronounced something like "mell-ee-tawn" — and they're the key ingredient in many healthy, hearty homemade dishes.

- 6 to 8 mirlitons
- 2 sticks of butter
- 2 cups of diced onion
- 2 cups of diced bellpepper
- 4 tablespoons of minced garlic
- 2 pounds of raw shrimp, peeled and diced
- 1 pound of diced ham
- 3 teaspoons of salt
- 2 teaspoons of black pepper
- 1 teaspoon of garlic powder
- 2 cups of Italian seasoned breadcrumbs

1. Place the mirlitons in a large pot and cover with water.

2. Boil the mirlitons until tender when pierced with a fork, about 30 minutes.

3. Drain off the water and set aside to cool completely.

4. Peel off the outer skin, cut open the mirlitons and remove the seeds. Discard the seeds and the skin.

5. Cut the mirliton meat in three-fourths-inch cubes. Set aside.

6. In a large Dutch oven or skillet, melt the butter over medium-high heat.

7. Sauté the onion and bellpepper for about five minutes, or until the onion is translucent.

8. Add garlic. Stir for a minute or two.

9. Add shrimp and ham, stir and simmer for three to five minutes or until the shrimp turn pink.

10. Add the mirlitons and mix well.

11. Reduce heat to medium-low and add salt, pepper and garlic powder. Cover and let simmer, stirring several times during the next 15 to 20 minutes.

12. Remove from the heat. Add the breadcrumbs one-half cup at a time, mixing well. You may have to adjust the amount of breadcrumbs if the mix appears to be too dry or too wet. If it appears to be too dry, add a little butter. The dressing is supposed to be moist, not runny.

13. Spoon the dressing into individual casserole dishes. Top with a light coating of breadcrumbs.

14. Bake uncovered for 30 minutes in a 350-degree oven.

Serves eight to ten.

– Kerri Diaz
Gretna (Jefferson Parish)

'Dirty Rice'

The livers and gizzards of chickens lend their color to this rice dish, making it appear dirty. Throughout south Louisiana, it's cheered as simply delicious.

- 1 pound of chicken livers
- 1 pound of chicken gizzards
- 10 tablespoons of vegetable oil
- 1 pound of ground pork
- 1½ cups of finely chopped bellpepper
- 1 cup of finely chopped celery
- 1 cup of finely chopped onion
- Salt and black pepper, to taste
- 4 cups of cooked long-grain rice
- Chopped spring onions

1. Chop the livers and gizzards separately; set aside.

2. Heat the oil in a skillet until almost smoking.

3. Add the ground pork to the skillet and stir to break up lumps.

4. Add the gizzards, cover and cook for 10 minutes.

5. Add the vegetables and cook over high heat for another 10 minutes.

6. Add the seasonings and stir, scraping up the browned particles that stick to the bottom of the skillet.

7. Add the rice and cook, stirring for about five minutes, then add the chopped chicken livers and cook five minutes more.

8. Sprinkle with spring onions.

Seves 10 to 12.

– John DeMers
New Orleans

Crabmeat Casserole

T. Pittari's Restaurant operated in New Orleans for 89 years, many of them in its location at South Claiborne Ave. and Milan St. Locals and tourists alike packed the place to enjoy some of the best Italian food this side of the Atlantic. This dish, shown on the menu as Hot Crabmeat a la Pittari, was, and is, a memorable appetizer.

- 3 tablespoons of olive oil, divided
- 1/2 cup of breadcrumbs
- 2 tablespoons of finely chopped garlic
- 1/8 tablespoon of salt
- 1/8 teaspoon of white pepper
- 3 tablespoons of fresh chopped parsley, divided
- 2 ounces of grated Romano cheese
- 8 ounces of back fin lump crabmeat, picked over for shells and cartilage

1. Put two tablespoons of olive oil into a small skillet and heat over low to medium heat.

2. Add breadcrumbs and mix thoroughly.

3. Add garlic, salt, pepper, two tablespoons of parsley and Romano cheese. Remove from heat and marinate for about five minutes.

4. Place some of the breadcrumb mixture in two small casserole dishes. Place crabmeat on top of the breadcrumb mixture; top with more breadcrumb mixture and a sprinkling of olive oil.

5. Bake uncovered for 15 minutes at 325 degrees.

6. Top with a sprinkling of fresh chopped parsley, about a half tablespoon per casserole. Serve with hot French bread.

Serves two.

– Tom Pittari Sr.
T. Pittari's Restaurant (1895 - 1984)
New Orleans

153

Mirliton Casserole

New Orleans folks love casseroles, especially casseroles made with their favorite local vegetables. This is one dish anyone's mamma would be proud to serve on a Sunday.

- 8 mirlitons
- ½ gallon of water
- 6 tablespoons of butter
- 3 cloves of garlic, minced
- 1 cup of chopped onion
- ½ cup of chopped shallots (green onions)
- 2 pounds of medium-size raw shrimp, peeled and deveined
- 1 teaspoon of cayenne pepper
- Salt and black pepper, to taste
- 4 tablespoons of all-purpose flour
- 1 cup of milk
- 1 egg
- 2 teaspoons of chopped parsley
- ½ cup of buttered fine breadcrumbs

1. Peel mirlitons, remove seeds, then cut in medium-sized cubes.

2. Fill a large stockpot with water, add salt and mirliton and simmer in salted water until tender, about 45 minutes. Drain and mash mirlitons until smooth.

3. Heat butter in a large skillet over medium-high heat. Sauté garlic, onion, shallots and shrimp 10 to 15 minutes. Stir-in cayenne pepper, salt and black pepper, to taste.

4. Sprinkle flour over the mixture in the skillet and stir well. Cook on medium heat and continue to stir until thick and bubbly. Remove from heat and cool.

5. Add milk, egg and parsley and stir mixture thoroughly.

6. Place mixture in a casserole dish and top with buttered breadcrumbs.

7. Bake uncovered at 375 degrees for 25 minutes.

Serves 10.

– Cheryl Lemoine
Martin Wine Cellar
Uptown New Orleans and Metairie

Sweet Potato Casserole

Sweet potatoes (usually called "yams" around New Orleans) are a classic side dish for baked chicken or baked turkey.

- 3 pounds of sweet potatoes
- ¼ cup of unsalted butter
- 1 tablespoon of ground cinnamon
- 1½ cups of dark brown sugar
- 1 tablespoon of orange zest

1. Peel the potatoes and cut into one-inch cubes.

2. Cover with water, bring to a boil, and cook about 30 minutes.

3. While they are cooking, combine the other ingredients in a bowl and blend together with a fork.

4. When potatoes are done, drain the liquid and mix potatoes with the sugar mixture.

5. Pour this mixture into a baking pan.

6. Cover and bake in a 350-degree oven for 30 minutes.

Serves eight.

Eggplant & Tomato Casserole

Fresh eggplants and tomatoes are abundant in the New Orleans area, in grocery stores and at farmers' markets, including the French Market in the Quarter. This easy-to-prepare dish is but one of the many ways to use these nutritious foods.

- 1 large eggplant, sliced thin
- 2 large tomatoes, sliced thin
- 1 can (24 oz.) of artichoke hearts, drained and sliced thin
- 6 ounces of olive oil
- 1 cup of Italian breadcrumbs
- 1½ cups of mozzarella cheese, grated

1. Preheat oven to 350 degrees.

2. Grease a small casserole dish.

3. Lay down one layer of vegetables, drizzle with some of the olive oil, breadcrumbs and cheese. Continue to layer until all ingredients are used up. Make sure the final layer is cheese and breadcrumbs.

4. Bake uncovered until eggplant is tender, 40 to 45 minutes.

Serves six to eight.

Mardi Gras float moves through downtown New Orleans during the Rex Parade.

History Of The
King Cake

The King Cake, or *Gateau du Roi*, dates back to 12th century France, where the cake was baked on the eve of the Epiphany – the church feast day which commemorates the three kings' visit to the Christ child, 12 days after his birth. A small token was hidden in the cake as a surprise for the finder.

French settlers brought the custom of the King Cake to Louisiana in the 18th century. It remained associated with the Epiphany until the middle of the 19th century, when it became an elaborate Mardi Gras custom. King Cakes were first associated with Mardi Gras by the Twelfth Night Revelers in New Orleans during the 1870 celebration. The cake, a circular or oval-shaped pastry decorated in bright colors representing a bejeweled crown, was baked with a golden bean inside for the ladies of the court. The lady whose slice contained the bean was crowned queen of the festivities. Thus began the Mardi Gras King Cake tradition.

Eventually, plastic babies were used in the King Cake as it became an integral part of the tradition of Mardi Gras. Today, family, friends and businesses have their own King Cake parties. Whoever gets the piece of cake with the plastic baby hosts the next King Cake party, or buys or bakes the next cake.

King Cake colors – purple, green and gold – are a common sight during Mardi Gras season. In 1872, King Rex, the king of New Orleans' carnival, selected those shades as the official colors of Mardi Gras. Purple represents justice, green signifies faith and gold stands for power. These colors are featured at every Mardi Gras celebration in Louisiana.

King Cake

- ½ cup of warm water (110 to 115 degrees)
- 2 (¼-ounce) packages of active dry yeast
- 2 teaspoons of sugar and 1/2 cup of sugar
- 4 cups of all-purpose flour, unsifted
- 1 teaspoon of allspice
- 2 teaspoons of salt
- 1 teaspoon of freshly grated lemon zest
- ½ cup of warm milk
- 5 egg yolks
- 1 stick of butter plus 2 tablespoons, softened
- 1 teaspoon of cinnamon
- 1 egg slightly beaten with 1 tablespoon
  of milk to make egg wash
- 1 one-inch plastic baby doll
- Icing (Recipe follows)

1. In a small, shallow mixing bowl, combine the warm water, yeast and two teaspoons of sugar. Allow the sugar and yeast to rest together for about three minutes, then mix thoroughly.

2. Set the bowl in a warm place until the yeast bubbles and the mixture nearly doubles in size, about 10 minutes.

3. In a separate large mixing bowl, combine three and one-half cups of flour, one-half cup of sugar, allspice and salt. Sift into a larger bowl. Stir-in lemon zest.

4. Make a hole in the center of the flour mixture and pour in the yeast mixture and a half of a cup of warm milk. Add egg yolks.

5. Using a wooden spoon, slowly combine dry ingredients with the yeast/milk mixture.

6. When mixture is smooth, add butter one tablespoon at a time and beat thoroughly. After all butter is added, continue to beat for two minutes or until the dough can be formed into a medium soft ball.

(Continued on next page)

7. Place ball of dough on a lightly floured surface and knead. During the kneading process add as much as another half cup of flour, one tablespoon at a time. When dough is no longer sticky, knead another 10 minutes, or until the dough is shiny and elastic.

8. Place dough back in the large mixing bowl that has a coating of butter. Coat the outside of the ball.

9. Cover the bowl with a thick kitchen towel. Place bowl in a draft-free area for one and one-half hours or until dough doubles in volume.

10. Coat a large baking sheet with butter.

11. Remove dough from bowl and place on a lightly floured surface. Using your fist, punch dough down with a heavy blow.

12. Sprinkle cinnamon over the top, pat and form dough into a circle — like a wreath.

13. Place the wreath of dough on the buttered baking sheet and complete the circle.

14. Cover dough with a towel and set it in a draft-free spot for 45 minutes, or until the dough doubles in volume.

15. Preheat oven to 375 degrees. Brush top and sides of cake with egg wash and bake on the middle oven rack for 25 to 30 minutes, until golden brown.

16. Remove and place on a wire rack to cool. At this time you can hide the plastic baby in the cake by pushing it into the cake from underneath.

17. Ice the cake according to the following directions.

ICING

- 3 cups of confectioner's sugar
- ¼ cup of lemon juice
- 3 to 6 tablespoons of water
- 4 tablespoons of green sugar sprinkles
- 4 tablespoons of purple sugar sprinkles
- 4 tablespoons of yellow sugar sprinkles

1. Combine confectioner's sugar, lemon juice and three tablespoons of water, then mix until smooth. If icing is too stiff, add more water until the icing is easily spread.

2. Coat the top of the cooled cake with icing.

3. Immediately sprinkle the colored sugars in sections, alternating colors. There should be about two green sections, two purple and two yellow.

– Rhonda Findley
New Orleans

Bananas Foster

New Orleans' most famous dessert was created by one of New Orleans' most famous restaurants, Brennan's. Owen Brennan asked his chef, Paul Blange, to create a new recipe using bananas as the key ingredient. Why bananas? At the time, in the 1950s, New Orleans was the major port of entry for bananas shipped from South and Central America. Mr. Brennan named the recipe after his good friend, Richard Foster, head of the New Orleans Crime Commission, which was passionately striving to clean up the French Quarter. This recipe first appeared in Holiday *Magazine and since has become synonymous with Brennan's Restaurant and New Orleans.*

- ¼ cup of butter
- 1 cup of brown sugar
- ½ teaspoon of ground cinnamon
- ¼ cup of banana liqueur
- 5 whole ripe bananas, peeled, cut in half and cut lengthwise
- ¼ cup of dark rum
- 5 scoops of vanilla ice cream

1. In a large skillet over low heat, combine the butter, sugar and cinnamon. Stir until the sugar dissolves.

2. Stir-in the banana liqueur. Add the bananas. Continue to cook until the bananas soften and begin to brown, about three minutes.

3. Slowly add the rum to the hot pan. Continue to cook until the rum is hot. Very carefully tip the pan to ignite the rum. (Or you can use a long-handled lighter to ignite the rum.) Continue to cook until the flame subsides, about one minute.

4. Divide the ice cream scoops into four serving bowls. Top with four banana slices and spoon the sauce over the top. Serve immediately.

Serves four.

– Brennan's Restaurant
French Quarter, New Orleans

Cherries Jubilee

Maybe Bananas Foster found its inspiration in flaming Cherries Jubilee, created by Auguste Escoffier in honor of Queen Victoria's Diamond Jubilee. Only Mr. Brennan and Chef Blange of Brennan's Restaurant know the answer to that. This dish is very simple and quick.

- 16 ounces of cherry pie filling
- ½ cup of brandy
- 4 scoops of vanilla ice cream

1. Heat cherries in a small saucepan over medium heat.

2. In another small saucepan, heat brandy on low heat. (The brandy won't flame unless it is heated.)

3. Pour heated brandy over the warm cherries and ignite, using a long-handled stick lighter.

4. Place the ice cream into serving dishes and divide the warmed cherries equally among the dishes.

Serves four.

Bread Pudding
with Whiskey Sauce

With all the good French bread from places like Binder's Bakery and Gendusa Bakery, it would be a shame to let any of it go to waste. We can thank the ingenious cooks who thought to put it to good use by making bread pudding.

- 1 loaf of day-old French bread
- 3 pints of whole milk
- 1 pint of half-and-half
- 3 eggs
- 2 cups of sugar
- 2 tablespoons of vanilla extract
- 2 teaspoons of allspice
- 1 teaspoon of grated nutmeg
- ½ teaspoon of ground cinnamon
- 1 cup of raisins
- 3 tablespoons of melted butter
- Whiskey Sauce (Recipe follows.)

1. Preheat oven to 325 degrees.

2. Tear bread into half-inch chunks. Put bread in a large mixing bowl. Pour milk and half-and-half over the bread. Mix bread and milk thoroughly by squeezing with your hands. Allow milk to soak through for about 20 minutes.

3. In a separate mixing bowl, combine eggs, sugar, vanilla extract, allspice, nutmeg, cinnamon and raisins. Mix thoroughly.

4. Pour egg mixture over bread and mix thoroughly.

5. Pour melted butter into a heavy-bottom baking pan. Pour bread mixture in baking pan and make an even layer. If you like, you can add a dusting of cinnamon and sugar.

6. Bake for 40 minutes, or until bread pudding is firm. Remove from oven and cool.

7. To serve, cut off a square, top with Whiskey Sauce and heat under a broiler.

WHISKEY SAUCE

- 1 cup of sugar
- 1 cup of butter
- 1 egg, beaten
- 2 ounces of Southern Comfort whiskey

1. Cream sugar and butter together. Heat in a double boiler until fully blended.

2. Add egg slowly and whip continuously to prevent egg from cooking.

3. Remove from heat and allow to cool. Add Southern Comfort and mix thoroughly.

Note: You can substitute rum for the whiskey. Add one-eighth cup of fresh squeezed orange juice and the flavors will really pop out!

Mile-High Ice Cream Pie

The long-departed Caribbean Room at the Pontchartrain Hotel contributed this chilly knockout to the list of New Orleans' all-time favorite desserts.

- 1½ pints of vanilla ice cream
- 1½ pints of chocolate ice cream
- ½ pint of strawberry ice cream
- ½ pint of peppermint ice cream
- 1 baked and cooled pie crust
- 8 egg whites
- ½ teaspoon of vanilla
- ¼ teaspoon of cream of tartar
- ½ cup of sugar
- Chocolate Sauce (Recipe follows)

1. Layer ice cream, one flavor after another, in the pie shell.

2. Beat egg whites with vanilla and cream of tartar, gradually adding sugar until stiff and glossy.

3. Spread meringue over ice cream to seal with edge of pie crust.

4. Broil for about 30 seconds, just enough to brown the meringue.

5. Freeze for several hours, preferably overnight. When ready to serve, drizzle Chocolate Sauce over each slice of pie.

CHOCOLATE SAUCE
- 2 squares of German sweet chocolate
- 2 squares of unsweetened chocolate
- ½ cup of sugar
- ½ cup of cream, divided

1. Melt chocolates with the sugar and one-fourth cup of the cream in the top of a double boiler. Stir until blended and thick.

2. Add enough cream so that the sauce will pour.

– Pontchartrain Hotel
New Orleans

Crème Brulée

A very popular dessert of set custard with a caramelized sugar topping is what the English call Burnt Cream. Patrick VanHoorebeek, the maitre d' at the Bistro at the Maison de Ville for many years, speaks fondly of this succulent dessert: "We here have the second-best crème brulée in the city of New Orleans. We're still looking for the best!"

- 1 pint of heavy cream
- ½ vanilla bean, scraped
- 5 large egg yolks, whisked thoroughly
- Pinch of salt
- ¼ cup and 1 tablespoon of superfine sugar
- Light brown granulated sugar

1. In a medium-size sauce pan over medium heat, bring cream to a boil, add vanilla bean scrapings and boil for 30 seconds.

2. Whisk egg yolks, salt and sugar together in a heavy-bottom stainless steel mixing bowl. Pour hot cream over egg yolks and whisk together.

3. Return cream mixture to pan and continue to cook on low heat until cream begins to thicken enough to coat a metal spoon. Remove from heat and transfer equal amounts to ramekins or small ovenproof custard cups.

4. Add about one-half inch of water to a deep baking pan large enough to accommodate the custard cups. Bake for about 15 minutes in a 350-degree oven. (Do not over-bake. Do not let the water in the pan boil.)

5. Remove from oven, cool, and chill overnight in the refrigerator.

6. Just prior to serving, sprinkle tops of custard with a light layer of brown sugar and, using a small torch, caramelize the sugar. The sugar will turn dark brown, bubble and form a crisp layer. Be careful not to burn the sugar.

Creole Macaroons

There are many variations on this incredible cookie. They can be soft or crunchy and flavored with anything from the classic coconut to coffee, dried cherries and liquors. Just as varied as the ingredients are the stories of the cookie's origin. We know the Italians created it, and it seems that the French perfected their own versions. It is no wonder the cookie is popular in New Orleans, since French and Italian influences are heavy here.

- 1½ cups of superfine sugar
- 2½ cups of ground almonds
- 4 egg whites
- 1/8 teaspoon of salt
- 1/2 teaspoon of cream of tartar

1. Preheat oven to 400 degrees. Line baking sheets with parchment baking paper.

2. Combine sugar and ground almonds.

3. In a non-reactive stainless steel or copper bowl, whip egg whites with salt and cream of tartar until the egg whites form soft peaks.

4. Fold-in sugar mixture to fully incorporate.

5. Spoon the cookie mixture onto the baking pan one tablespoon at a time.

6. Bake for 20 minutes or until cookies are golden brown.

Blackberry Cobbler

Lots of New Orleanians either have blackberry bushes on or near their property, or they know where to find some real fast. This cobbler is only one of several desserts that sing ole Gershwin's "Summertime... and the livin' is easy" to so many.

- 2 prepared pie crusts, rolled out flat
- 1 quart of blackberries
- 2 cups of sugar
- ¾ pound of butter
- 1 cup of heavy cream, whipped

1. Preheat oven to 325 degrees.

2. Line sides of a two-quart baking dish with one-half of one sheet of the pastry.

3. Cover the baking dish with one-half of the berries, sugar and butter; then cut one-half sheet of pastry into small pieces and scatter them across the top of the berries.

4. Add remaining half of berries, sugar and butter.

5. Place remaining sheet of pastry on top.

6. Cut holes in pastry and bake until golden brown, about one hour.

7. In a bowl, whip the heavy cream until light and fluffy.

8. Serve cobbler squares hot with a dollop of whipped cream on each.

Serves six to eight.

Divinity Fudge

- 2½ cups of sugar
- ½ cup of light corn syrup
- ¼ teaspoon of salt
- ½ cup of water
- 2 egg whites
- 1 teaspoon of vanilla

1. In a heavy two-quart saucepan, combine the sugar, corn syrup, salt and water.

2. Cook over medium heat, stirring until the sugar dissolves and the mixture reaches the hard-ball stage (260 degrees on a candy thermometer).

3. Meanwhile, beat the egg whites at high speed until stiff peaks form.

4. Gradually and steadily, add the sugar mixture and vanilla into the egg whites and beat with an electric mixer until the candy holds it shape, about five minutes.

5. Quickly drop by the teaspoonful onto waxed paper. Cool completely.

Makes about 40 candies.

– Marcelle Bienvenu

Rice Pudding

When all else fails, south Louisiana has lots of rice. New Orleanians may have learned this recipe from the Spaniards way back when.

- 3 cups of cooked rice, preferably day-old
- 1 cup of heavy cream
- 1 stick of butter
- ¾ cup of sugar
- 1 teaspoon of vanilla extract
- ½ cup of raisins
- 3 eggs, beaten
- 6 egg yolks, beaten
- ½ teaspoon of ground cinnamon
- ½ teaspoon of ground nutmeg

1. Combine the rice with the cream in a large pan and bring to a boil, stirring until the cream has been absorbed.

2. Stir-in the butter, sugar, vanilla and raisins.

3. Combine eggs, egg yolks, cinnamon and nutmeg in a bowl and carefully stir-in some of the rice mixture. Then pour this mixture into the pan with the rest of the rice mixture and stir.

4. Pour this into a buttered two-quart baking dish or casserole.

5. Bake at 350 degrees for 30 minutes.

Serves eight to ten.

Pecan Pie

We in New Orleans share our love for pecan pie with quite a few other parts of the Deep South. But we always like to say ours is the best, anyway.

- 2 cups of sugar
- ½ teaspoon of salt
- 6 eggs
- 1½ tablespoons of melted butter
- ¾ cup of heavy whipping cream
- ¾ cup of dark Karo brand syrup
- ½ teaspoon of vanilla extract
- 2 cups of chopped pecans
- 2 unbaked 10-inch pie crusts

1. Preheat the oven to 350 degrees.

2. Sift together the sugar and salt in a medium bowl, then beat-in the eggs, melted butter, cream, Karo syrup, and vanilla.

3. Stir-in the pecans and pour the mixture into the pie shells.

4. Bake until set, about 25 minutes.

5. Allow to cool before serving.

Serves 10 to 12.

Pecan Pralines

The perfect candy! Do try to watch pralines being made whenever you get the chance. It's amazing that something so wonderful just gets poured out to cool, praline after praline. Oh yes, of course, it's praw-leens, not pray-leens!

- 2 cups of light brown sugar
- 1/2 cup of heavy whipping cream
- 1 tablespoon of butter
- 2 teaspoons of vanilla extract, divided
- 1/4 teaspoon of salt
- 1½ cups of shelled pecans

1. In a large stainless steel pot, combine sugar, cream, butter, one teaspoon of vanilla and salt. Cook until mixture reaches the soft-ball stage, about 235 degrees. (You can check this by cooking with a candy thermometer.)

2. Add pecans and stir before removing from heat.

3. Add second teaspoon of vanilla.

4. Drop mixture by the spoonful on buttered wax paper. Cool until the candy hardens.

Note: Make sure to cook in a dry area without a lot of humidity.

Makes about a dozen and a half.

– Elayne Angel
French Quarter, New Orleans

Bourbon Street is one of the most famous streets in the world. It is alive with throngs of people well into the wee hours of the morning, especially on the weekends.

Adult Beverages

Hurricane

This must be the most popular drink in the history of New Orleans, a tropical-style mix of bright fruit juice and both light and dark rum. It was concocted in the 1940s during World War II at Pat O'Brien's, in the French Quarter. Then it was named "The Hurricane" when bartenders started serving the drink in a tall glass shaped like a hurricane lamp. The original Pat O'Brien's was founded in 1933, with other such bars opening in Cancun, Orlando, Memphis and San Antonio, starting in the early 1990s.

- 1 ounce of light rum
- 1 ounce of dark rum
- 1 ounce of amaretto
- 6 ounces of orange juice
- 6 ounces of pineapple juice
- 1 teaspoon of freshly squeezed lemon juice
- 1 dash of grenadine syrup
- 1 orange slice, for garnish
- 1 maraschino cherry with stem, for garnish

1. Fill a cocktail shaker with crushed ice.

2. Pour light rum, dark rum, amaretto, orange juice, pineapple and lemon juice over ice. Cover and shake well until thoroughly chilled.

3. Pour drink into a large specialty glass or a traditional Hurricane-style glass.

4. Top with grenadine and garnish with the orange slice and cherry.

Serves one.

– Candice Lamb
The Bywater District
New Orleans

Mint Julep

Let no number of European touches confuse you — New Orleans is part of the Deep South. If you ever want to feel like a rich sugar planter out along the River Road, make yourself one of these mint juleps.

- 4 sprigs of fresh mint
- 1 teaspoon of sugar
- Splash of water
- 2½ to 3 ounces of bourbon

1. In either a silver mint julep glass or a tall glass, crush mint leaves with sugar.

2. Add a splash of water and fill glass to the top with finely crushed ice. Shake or stir until a frost begins to develop on the outside of the glass.

3. Add bourbon, mix lightly and serve.

Makes one serving.

– Adam Peltz
Faubourg Marigny District
New Orleans

Gin Fizz

A bartender named Henry Ramos made this drink famous. In many quarters it's still called a Ramos Gin Fizz.

- 1½ ounces of gin
- 2 drops of orange flower water
- 1 egg white
- 1 tablespoon of simple syrup
- ½ teaspoon of lemon juice
- 2 ounces of half-and-half
- 2 ounces of milk

1. Combine all ingredients with ice in a shaker.

2. Shake vigorously for 30 seconds, then pour over ice cubes in a chilled champagne glass.

Sazerac

This popular cocktail was created in the mid-1800s at the Sazerac Bar, which was later incorporated into the Roosevelt Hotel, which is today the Fairmont.

- 2 ounces of rye whiskey
- 1 teaspoon of simple syrup (Made by combining equal parts of sugar and water)
- 3 dashes of Peychaud's bitters
- Splash of water
- 2 dashes of Herbsaint liqueur
- Lemon twist

1. Combine the whiskey, simple syrup, bitters and water with ice.

2. Sprinkle the Herbsaint into an Old Fashion glass just to coat, then pour it out.

3. Strain the whiskey mixture into the glass and add the lemon twist.

Café Brulot

In Old Guard restaurants around the French Quarter, this is a labor-intensive delight, performed pyrotechnically by the best waiters in each house. Local TV legends Bob and Jan Carr here share a less snazzed-up version that will please any and all nonetheless.

- 1 skin of an orange, cut in a continuous strand and laced with whole cloves
- 1 skin of a lemon, cut in a continuous strand and laced with whole cloves
- 1 cup of brandy
- 1 lump of sugar per serving
- 1 whole cinnamon stick, broken into pieces
- 1 quart of hot, hot strong coffee

1. In a brulot bowl, place peelings, brandy, sugar and cinnamon.

2. Carefully ignite the brandy using a long-stem match.

3. Let this burn for a minute, then snuff out the flame by pouring in the coffee.

4. Voila! You are ready to serve.

Serves 10 to 12 in demitasse.

– Bob and Jan Carr
French Quarter, New Orleans
(Recipe created by Mrs. Edward Preston Munson.)

Index

183

184

JOHN DeMERS is a New Orleans native and author of 26 published books, including *New Orleans by the Bowl*, *The New Orleans Seafood Cookbook*, and *The Food Lovers' Guide to Texas*. He is editor and publisher of the new *Texas Foodlover* magazine and co-host of the weekly Houston radio show, "Dish."

After graduating from LSU in Baton Rouge with a Bachelor's then a Master's Degree in journalism, he was a globetrotting reporter and Food Editor for United Press International, eating his way through 126 foreign countries before concentrating on the foods of home. He has served as food and wine editor of *New Orleans* magazine, as a weekly commentator on WYES-TV's "Steppin' Out," and as co-host of New Orleans food and wine radio shows.

RHONDA FINDLEY is a freelance food and wine writer and is one of the nation's leading broadcasters on the subject of New Orleans cuisine. A resident of the Crescent City, she has co-hosted food and wine radio shows in both Houston and New Orleans. She earned a Bachelor's Degree in journalism from the University of Arkansas and co-authored a number of books, including *The Food Lovers' Guide to Texas*, *Houston Unleashed* and *New Orleans Unleashed*.

Regional Books
About *Intriguing* South Louisiana

The Truth About The Cajuns

A 120-page paperback book that describes the French-Acadian, or Cajun, people with the accuracy and dignity to which they are entitled – contrary to the shallow, stereotyping manner in which they have been depicted by many of the news media. This controversial book sets the record straight about the Cajun people and their culture. Illustrated with maps and photos. (Author: Trent Angers. ISBN: 0-925417-29-7. Price: $11.95)

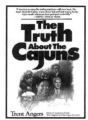

Louisiana's French Heritage

A 192-page hardcover book about the French contribution to the colonization of the New World. It describes the settlement of the Acadian Peninsula, the discovery and exploration of the Mississippi River, the development of the first Louisiana colony and the exile of the French-Acadians from Canada. Illustrated with maps and historical drawings. (Author: Truman Stacey. ISBN: 0-925417-02-5. Price: $15.95)

From Small Bits of Charcoal: *The Life & Works Of A Cajun Artist*

This 190-page hardcover book is the autobiography of pen-and-ink artist Floyd Sonnier (1933-2002) of Lafayette, La. Written and illustrated by Mr. Sonnier, the book tells the story of growing up as a French-speaking Cajun in rural south Louisiana in the 1940s and '50s. It is also a testament to his love of his French-Acadian, or Cajun, culture and heritage. (ISBN: 0-925417-46-7. Price: $59.95)

Dudley LeBlanc: A Biography

A 104-page softcover book about Dudley LeBlanc, the most famous Cajun of all time, and unquestionably one of Louisiana's most unforgettable characters. The political leader of the Cajun people in the 1930s, '40s, '50s and '60s, "Coozan Dud" also invented and promoted HADACOL into the best-selling patent medicine in America in its time. (Author: Trent Angers. ISBN: 0-925417-12-2. Price: $9.95)

Dreaming Impossible Dreams:
Reflections of an Entrepreneur

This 176-page autobiography is the rags-to-riches story of multimillionaire philanthropist E.J. Ourso of Donaldsonville, Louisiana, the man for whom the LSU Business School is named. It reveals how Ourso acquired 56 businesses in 48 years – the first 25 with no money down. A testament to the effectiveness of the American free enterprise system, the book chronicles Ourso's life beginning with his early years as a salesman. It reveals his secrets to the acquisition of wealth. (Author: E.J. Ourso with Dan Marin. Hardcover ISBN: 0-925417-42-4, Price: $22.95; Softcover ISBN: 0-925417-43-2, Price: $14.95)

The New Orleans Saints:
25 Years of Heroic Effort

A set of 2 hardcover books (112 and 184 pages) describes the colorful history of the Saints from 1967 thru 1991, featuring Tom Dempsey, Archie Manning, Bobby Hebert, Dalton Hilliard, Morten Andersen, "The Dome Patrol" and many more. Illustrated with photos. (ISBN: 0-925417-09-2 and 0-925417-11-4. Price: $25 for the set)

The Top 100 CAJUN Recipes Of All Time

A 48-page saddle-stitched soft cover book containing 100 recipes selected by the editors of *Acadiana Profile*, "The Magazine of the Cajun Country." For example, Boudin, Couche Couche, Maque Choux, Mirliton, Crawfish Etouffee, Chicken Fricassee, Pralines–the classics of South Louisiana cuisine. (ISBN: 0-925417-20-3. Price: $7.95)

The Top 100 NEW ORLEANS Recipes Of All Time

A 192-page hardcover book containing 100 of the recipes that have helped to make New Orleans food world-famous. For example, Shrimp Creole, Red Beans & Rice, Blackened Redfish, Oyster Loaf, Muffaletta, Beignets, Café au Lait and King Cake. (ISBN: 0-925417-51-3. Price: $14.95)

Cajun Cooking For Beginners

A 48-page saddle-stitched soft cover book that teaches the basics of authentic Cajun cooking. It contains about 50 simple, easy-to-follow recipes; cooking tips and hints; a glossary of Cajun food terms, such as roux, gumbo, jambalaya and etouffee; and definitions of basic cooking terms, such as beat, blend, broil, sauté and simmer. (Author: Marcelle Bienvenu. ISBN: 0-925417-23-8. Price: $7.95)

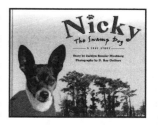